MIX
Papier aus verantwortungsvollen Quellen
Paper from responsible sources
FSC® C105338

Christian Schießl

Value Stocks beat Growth Stocks

An empirical Analysis for the German Stock Market

Anchor Academic Publishing

Schießl, Christian: Value Stocks beat Growth Stocks: An empirical Analysis for the German Stock Market. Hamburg, Anchor Academic Publishing 2013

Buch-ISBN: 978-3-95489-069-9
PDF-eBook-ISBN: 978-3-95489-569-4
Druck/Herstellung: Anchor Academic Publishing, Hamburg, 2013

Bibliografische Information der Deutschen Nationalbibliothek:
Die Deutsche Nationalbibliothek verzeichnet diese Publikation in der Deutschen Nationalbibliografie; detaillierte bibliografische Daten sind im Internet über http://dnb.d-nb.de abrufbar.

Bibliographical Information of the German National Library:
The German National Library lists this publication in the German National Bibliography. Detailed bibliographic data can be found at: http://dnb.d-nb.de

Table of contents

List of tables

List of figures

List of abbreviations

B/M	Book-to-market ratio
B/P	Book-to-price ratio
BE/ME	Book equity-to-market equity
bn	Billion
CAPM	Capital Asset Pricing Model
CDAX	"Composite Deutscher Aktien Index"
CEO	Chief Executive Officer
CPI	Consumer price index
D	Debt
D/E	Debt-to-equity ratio
D/P	Dividend yield
DAX	"Deutscher Aktien Index"
DCF	Discounted Cash Flow
DDM	Dividend Discount Model
DPS	Dividends per share
DY	Dividend yield
E	Equity
E/P	Earnings-to-price
g	Growth rate
GDP	Gross domestic product
IDW	"Institut der Wirtschaftsprüfer"
IPO	Initial public offering
M	Model
m	Million
Mom.	Momentum

MRP	Market risk-premium
NAV	Net asset value
NYSE	New York Stock Exchange
P/B	Price-to-book ratio
P/CF	Price-to-Cash-flow ratio
P/D	Price-dividend ratio
P/E	Price-to-earnings ratio
P/S	Price-to-sales ratio
PEG	Price-earnings-growth ratio
PF	Portfolio
PPI	Producer price index
R&D	Research and Development
REXP	„Renten-Performance Index“
Std.Dev.	Standard deviation
SME’s	Small- and medium- sized companies
t	Time
t	Tax-rate
t	T-statistics
U.K.	United Kingdom
U.S.	United States
YTM	Yield-to-maturity

List of symbols

$\propto_i$	Intercept in the regression analysis
β'	Factor loading
β_i	Measure of the systematic risk-premium
β_l	Levered beta factor
β_u	Unlevered beta factor
$b_0 \ldots b_3, t_{1,} t_2$	Vector of parameters describing the yield curve
BMS	Reversed size risk factor
$Cov(r_i, r_m)$	Covariance of the expected market return and stock i
$\varepsilon_p(t)$	Error term for portfolio p at time t.
$E(r_i)$	Expected return of stock i
$E(r_m)$	Expected return of the market portfolio
$E(r_m) - r_f$	Expected market risk premium
$F_{i,t}$	Vector of factor I for month t
HML	Fama and French risk factor for value companies
M1	Central bank money supply
m	Maturity at which the spot rate is calculated
$P_{i,\tau}$	Share price of stock i in month τ
$r_{i,\tau}$	Return of stock i in month τ
r_f	Risk-free or basic interest rate
RMRF	Market risk factor
SMB	Fama and French risk factor for Size
UMD	Risk factor for Momentum
$Var(r_m)$	Variance of the market return
y_f	Risk-free spot rate term structure

1. Introduction

1.1 Motivation

There has been an ongoing discussion for many years of whether value investing-, or growth investing strategies achieve higher stock market returns. Value firms can be defined as those that have a poor past performance and are expected to perform below average in the future, whereas growth firms as those that performed strongly in the past and are expected to have a high performance in the future. In literature value (growth) firms are characterized by low (high) price-to-earnings ratios [P/E], low (high) price-to-book ratios [P/B], low (high) price-to-cash-flow ratios [P/CF], low (high) price-to-sales ratios [P/S], and high (low) dividend yields [DY = D/P]. The rising academic interest in value and growth investment strategies can be traced back to the two seminal papers of Fama and French in 1992 and 1993. Their three-factor model containing additional risk premiums for "low minus high P/B stocks" and "small- minus big- sized stocks" meant a blow to the explanatory power of the Capital Asset Pricing Model (CAPM) of Sharpe (1964) and Lintner (1965) and rose the question of the "death" of the beta factor.[1] Based on the evidence from numerous empirical investigations on the P/B effect and related anomalies, the consensus has been evolved that value investing strategies, on average, outperform growth investing strategies and thus generate a value premium. Chan et al. (1991), for example, find significant value premiums for the Japanese market with the P/B ratio being the best proxy for expected stock returns.[2] Fama and French (1998) document that value stocks outperform growth stocks in 12 out of 13 major markets. They further test whether a global asset pricing model can explain stock returns and find that an international two-factor model does a good job.[3] However, Griffin (2002), amongst others, states that domestic factor models had a higher power to explain time-series variation in stock returns than a world factor model.[4] Beside the value premium proxies, a bulk of empirical research has been done on the size premium, i.e. that small companies, on average, perform better than big companies.[5] In addition, recent literature has shown a high interest in a technical firm characteristic – the Momentum factor.[6] Findings on these factors arouse the motivation to examine which trading strategies perform best for German stocks.

---

[1] See for example Fama and French (1996), p. 1947.
[2] See Chan et al. (1991), p. 1761.
[3] See Fama and French (1998), p. 1997.
[4] See Griffin (2002), p. 783.
[5] See for example Banz (1981).
[6] See for example Carhart (1997).

1.2. Structure and objective

Based on a "free of survivorship-bias" sample of German stocks listed at the Frankfurt stock exchange, the study investigates the ability of hedge portfolio formation structures, built of three value premium proxies (P/B, P/E, and DY), the size factor, and the technical momentum factor, to generate excess returns in the period 1992 to 2011. The study differs in three main aspects from common methodologies: First, financial firms are not excluded from the sample. Second, risk-factors are built from one-dimensional sorts, and not from double-sorts. And most important, third, all portfolios are rebalanced on a monthly basis, whereas common studies rearrange their portfolios on firm characteristics only once a year. These deviations should, in best, yield higher hedge returns in comparison to relevant studies.

The remainder is structured as follows: Section 2 gives an overview of characteristics and definitions that are associated with value and growth investing. Section 3 discusses the theoretical framework of asset pricing with the CAPM, the Fama and French three-factor model, and the Carhart extension. The most important determinants of expected stock returns are described in section 4. Related studies for the German stock market are presented in section 5. Before section 7 concludes, the empirical analysis is described in detail in section 6. Three main questions should be addressed:

1) Is there a value premium in the German market between 1992 and 2011, is there a reversed size premium like recent empirical findings[7] suggest, and do high momentum stocks perform better than low momentum stocks?
2) Is there a significant seasonal pattern in hedge portfolio returns?
3) The combination of which factors best explains expected stock returns?

[7] See for example van Dijk (2011).

2. Conceptual definition

2.1. Value investing

The principles of value investing can be traced back to the two fundamental books of Benjamin Graham – "Security Analysis", which he wrote in 1934 coauthored by David Dodd, and the "Intelligent Investor", which he wrote in 1949. Although Graham has not used the term to describe his approach, he is known as the father of value investing.[8] Graham's core principle remains the "margin of safety", i.e., a security should only be purchased, if its price is substantially below its intrinsic value.[9] The intrinsic value is the "actual value of a company or an asset based on an underlying perception of its true value including all aspects of the business, in terms of both tangible and intangible factors"[10]. Thus, value investors believe that the true value of a security is not reflected in its price. Value stocks tend to be cheap relative to their current intrinsic value. Market participants may not be willing to pay more for companies which are out of favor. Thus, the task of value investors is to indentify companies that are likely to manage a turnaround, leading to higher earnings and higher stock prices. To identify undervalued stocks, a comprehensive fundamental analysis has to be done.

John Burr Williams extended the concept of value investing by determining a company's intrinsic value through discounting its probable future cash flows.[11] Estimating future cash flows and the appropriate discount rate is difficult, takes some time and depends on realistic assumptions. Martin J Whitman (1999) lists some further properties of value investing:

- Value investing treats every accounting number or financial ratio equally and businesses are valued as wholes.
- The primary goal is to value a business independent of potential interests from passive minority investors.
- Macroeconomic factors like the Gross domestic product (GDP) or employment forecasts are not considered. The analysis aims only on the idiosyncratic factors which exert a long term influence on a company.
- The company analysis is strictly separated from market analysis.

[8] See Lowe (1996), p. 1.
[9] See Greenwald et al. (2001), p. 3.
[10] www.investopia.com, (http://www.investopedia.com/terms/i/intrinsicvalue.asp#axzz1x1cuQOjQ), as of 15.06.2012.
[11] See Cunningham (2004), p. 7.

- Value investing uses only financial analysis, no technical and chartist analyses.[12]

The measures of what defines a value company can usually be found in the balance sheet. Value companies have typically high assets in the form of tangibles like machines, real estate and inventory. They often belong to industries like auto manufacturing, timber and metal. These companies usually operate with very low profit margins. Thus, value companies are usually characterized by a strong balance sheet.

An easy way to determine the intrinsic value of a company and to make stocks comparable is the application of multiples. This concept is used in finance literature as well as in practice. The intrinsic or fair value of a company is determined by means of financial ratios. If the current market value is below the intrinsic value of a company, it seems to be worth to buy the stock. The intrinsic value is often used synonymous with the book value of a firm, or more exactly the net asset value (NAV). The NAV corresponds to the equity of the firm. The market value (price times number of outstanding shares) of the company divided by the book value (equity in the balance sheet) results in the financial ratio "price-to-book" (P/B). The lower this ratio, the cheaper is the stock in relation to its peer group. Further ratios of the value approach are a low price-to-earnings ratio (P/E), a low price-to-sales ratio (P/S), and a low price-to-cash-flow ratio (P/CF).[13] Thus, value managers invest mainly in companies with low valuations and stable earnings- and growth forecasts. Because of these attributes value investing is regarded as the appropriate investment style for defensive investors. At the moment, for example Volkswagen can be seen as a typical value company, trading at a P/B of 0.84 and a P/E of 2.9 in December 2011.[14]

2.2. Growth investing

Growth companies or glamour firms have a stronger past performance than the average company and are expected to perform very strong in the future.[15] According to Benjamin Graham "[t]he term "growth stock" is applied to one which has increased its per-share earnings in the past at well above the rate for common stocks generally and is expected to continue to do so in the future."[16] Growth investors believe that these high growth companies would enable them to outperform the stock-market in the long run. The market is willing to pay more for

[12] See Whitman (1999), pp. 3-5.
[13] See Fama and French (1998), p. 1975.
[14] Data are from Datastream request.
[15] See Ghargori et al. (2011), p. 2.
[16] Graham and Zweig (2003), p. 115.

growth stocks, since these are leading companies with the potential for fast earnings growth, and may thus be worth considerably more in the future. Philip A. Fisher is regarded the forerunner in the field of growth investing. Beside the fundamental analysis, he also focused on qualitative aspects of a company like management ability, risk management, innovation and business strategy. Intangible assets like the brand-name and the goodwill of a firm became important.[17] Fisher extended the number of value investing candidates by emphasizing that also cheap stocks can be unprofitable investments, in fact, if the stock trades below its intrinsic value because of bad management.[18]

Simultaneously, the high potential of growth stocks bears the danger that expectations will be disappointed. The demand for growth stocks arised, above all, in the late 1990s with the internet boom. There were numerous initial public offerings (IPO's) of companies with very high earnings growth expectations. In the German market, a well-known case is the case of EMTV. The German media company was issued on the "Neuer Markt" platform for a price of 35.50 Deutsche Mark (DM) (adjusted for various share splits: 0.35 EUR) in October 1997. In the beginning of 2000 the stock peaked at a price of 120 Euro (EUR). This meant a gain of over 30,000 percent since the IPO. In 1999, the company generated sales of DM 317 million (m) with 220 employees, whereas the market value exceeded DM 15 billion (bn).[19] At this point of time, EMTV was valued as high as the Deutsche Aktienindex (DAX)[20] company Lufthansa and had a very high P/S ratio of approximately 22. In the mid of 2000 the decline of the stock started and in April 2003 the Chief Executive Officers (CEO's) were convicted to pay high fines due to wrong presentations of the condition of the company. EMTV was not the only company that failed to achieve the high expectations. After the burst of the "dot-com bubble", a lot of companies of the so-called "New Economy" went bankrupt.
A similar phenomenon, happening at the moment, is the IPO of the social network Facebook. Since the first listing on May 18, the stock declined from USD 38 to USD 26.81[21], a minus of approximately 30 per cent. This means a decline in the market value of USD 34.5 bn in a few weeks.[22] On 7 June 2012, the company trades at a 2012 P/E of 49.27 and a 2013 P/E of 41.20.[23] These high ratios are reminiscent of the "Neue Markt" valuations.

---

[17] See Cunningham (2004), p. 10.
[18] See Cunningham (2004), p. 10.
[19] See Manager Magazin Online (2003), http://www.managermagazin.de/finanzen/artikel/0,2828,147003,00.html, as of 10.06.2012.
[20] The „Deutsche Aktienindex" (DAX) ist the index of the 30 largest German stocks.
[21] Closing price on 7 June 2012, source: www.onvista.de.
[22] See Eddy (2012), http://www.geekosystem.com/facebook-value/, as of 05.06.2012.
[23] These P/E ratios are average values of analyst's forecasts, see www.onvista.de.

A growth-oriented investor sets the future in the foreground. Not the current sales or earnings are important, but the expectation of strong sales- and earnings growth. Hence, growth stocks are characterized by high P/B ratios, high P/E ratios and low dividend yields. Growth stocks trade with a growth premium. An extreme example for growth investing would be the investment in a start-up company. These companies have typically a low amount of assets and often negative earnings, but have at the same time a high potential for growth. Positive examples of recent growth companies are Apple and Google. The future will show, if Facebook becomes a "second Google" or a "second EMTV".

2.3. Links between Value and Growth investing

Value stocks are considered to have a poor past performance and are expected to perform poorly in the future, whereas growth stocks performed strongly in the past and are expected to have a strong performance in the future. However, to draw this borderline and categorize stocks in either value or growth remains challenging in practice. The discrepancy between the price of a stock and its intrinsic value can make a value company into a growth stock and vice versa.[24] This phenomenon arises, for example, if a well established and saturated company discloses low or no earnings. If valued only by means of the P/E ratio, the company will be classified as a growth stock. Furthermore, classifications can change over time. A company that is now classified as a growth company can be classified as a value company within a few years. The other way round – the development from a value company to a growth company – is also possible, even if this is more difficult. A prominent representative can be seen in Apple. After starting as a growth company in 1981, the stock developed more and more to a value company in the 1990s, by means of a decline in the P/E ratio. However, since 2004 the P/E has risen again. Today analysts and financial experts are at odds with Apple to be labeled as growth stock or value stock.[25] Both, value and growth portfolio managers invest in Apple. This example shows again the difficulty of categorizing stocks into value and growth. Also Warren Buffet, the most famous student of Benjamin Graham and successful value investor said that the value and growth investment style are "joined at the hip"[26], since growth is always part of value investing. However, table 1 tries to summarize different characteristics of value and growth investing:

[24] See Martin et al. (2008), p. 15.
[25] See Bloch (2012), http://seekingalpha.com/article/325572-is-apple-a-growth-or-value-stock-who-cares, as of 16.06.2012.
[26] See Buffet, Warren (2003), Chairman's letter – 1992, http://www.berkshirehathaway.com/letters/1992.html, as of 16.06.2012.

Table 1: Characteristics of value and growth stocks

Value	Growth
Low price-to-earnings ratio (P/E)	High price-to-earnings ratio (P/E)
Low price-to-sales ratio (P/S)	High price-to-sales ratio (P/S)
Low price-to-cash-flow ratio (P/CF)	High price-to-cash-flow ratio (P/CF)
Low price-to-book-ratio (P/B)	High price-to-book-ratio (P/B)
Low, stable earnings growth	Longterm, high earnings growth
High dividend yield (DY)	No or lower dividend yield (DY)
Stable cash-flow	Fast growing cash-flow
Low debt-to-equity ratio (D/E)	High debt-to-equity ratio (D/E)
Good market position	High sales growth
High return on equity (ROE)	Low return on equity (ROE)
Earnings estimates (last 12 months)	Earnings estimates (upcoming 12 months)
Lower volatility	Higher volatility
Evaluation of the balance sheet	Evaluation of the income statement and profit margins
Typical industries: Auto manufacturers, metal, timber, paper companies	Typical industries: Technology, health-care, renewable energies

(Source: Own representation based on Naumer et al. (2009), p. 5)

3. Asset pricing theories

3.1. Capital Asset Pricing Model

The Capital Asset Pricing Model (CAPM) is still the most important tool in practice to determine the expected stock return or cost of equity of a specific company. The CAPM is a one-period equilibrium model which is based on the portfolio theory of Markowitz[27]. The model is based on several assumptions:[28]

- Investors are risk-averse and thus choose the portfolio with the lowest risk out of all portfolios with the same return, i.e. minimizing the volatility at a given expected value (all investors use Markowitz optimization).
- Any fraction of securities can be traded at any point of time and there are no short-selling restrictions.
- Investors are price-taker, i.e. investments have no influence on the market price.

[27] See Markowitz (1952).
[28] See Perridon and Steiner (1993), p. 250.

- There are no transaction costs and no taxes.
- Investors can borrow and lend money at the risk-free rate.
- Information is costless and available to everyone.
- All forms of securities can be traded.
- All market participants have homogenous expectations regarding returns, variances and covariances.
- Investors control risk through diversification.

According to the CAPM the expected return of a security i can be determined as a linear function of the firm's idiosyncratic beta factor (β):

$$E(r_i) = r_f + [E(r_m) - r_f] * \beta_i \qquad (3.1)$$

$$\beta_i = \frac{cov(r_j, r_m)}{var(r_m)} \qquad (3.2)$$

$E(r_i)$	=	Expected return of stock i
$E(r_m)$	=	Expected return of the market portfolio
r_f	=	risk-free or basic interest rate
$E(r_m) - r_f$	=	Market risk premium
$Cov(r_i, r_m)$	=	Covariance of the expected market return and stock i
$Var(r_m)$	=	Variance of the market return
β_i	=	Measure of the systematic risk-premium

Thus, according to the CAPM only three factors are necessary to calculate the expected stock return: the risk-free interest rate, the market risk-premium and the beta factor. Methods, how these components can be derived, are discussed in the following.

3.1.1. Risk-free interest rate

The basic interest rate is the return of a risk-free investment with identical terms at the valuation point.[29] Since there is no risk-free debtor in a theoretical context, the risk-free interest rate is approximated by the returns[30] of high-rated[31] government bonds. In this context, in particular, two issues are discussed in literature: First, the question of which market data should be used – historical average returns of government bonds, the return that applies on the date of valuation, or the interest of zero-coupon bonds (spot rates). And second that there is no risk-

[29] See Drukarczyk (2003), p. 352.
[30] The term return corresponds to the yield-to-maturity (YTM) of a bond.
[31] High-rated government bonds are bonds with an AAA rating like German government bonds.

free comparison security with an endless maturity.[32] Most valuation approaches assume an infinite maturity, whereas government bonds are only available up to a maturity of 30 years.

Figure 1 illustrates the development of German government bond yields with different maturities. It is obvious that long-term bonds should have higher returns than short-term bonds, since they face a higher interest rate risk. In rare cases short-term bonds pay a higher interest than long-term bonds. This situation is called inverse yield curve and occurs, if the market expects decreasing interests in the future. Whereas average yields accounted for about seven per cent in 1994, a ten-year German government bond pays only 1.45 percent on 7 June 2012, and the one-year German government bond is close to zero with 0.03 percent.[33] Figure 2 shows the yield curves of German government bonds, Eurobonds (red line) and Corporate bonds with differing ratings. Due to these historical low yields of German government bonds, in particular, in comparison to Eurobonds, it can be questioned, whether the derivation of the risk-free interest rate only out of German government bonds can be maintained.

Figure 1: Development of German government bond yields with different maturities

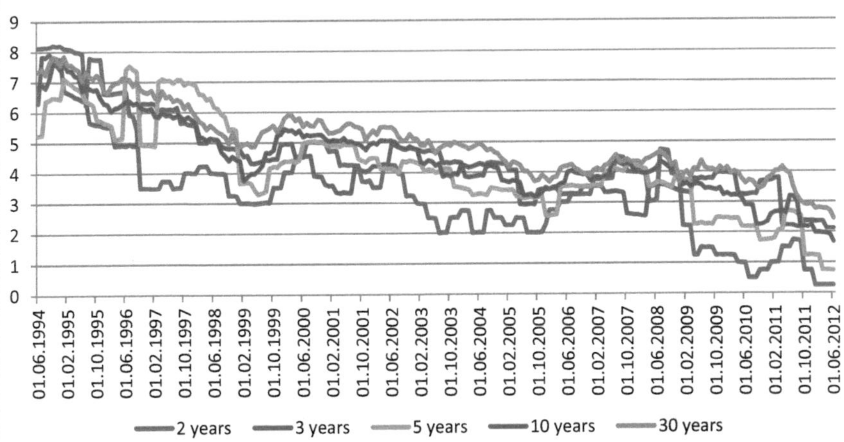

(Source: Own representation, Data from Thomson Reuters Datastream)

[32] See Reese, Wiese (2005), p. 4.
[33] See figure 2.

Figure 2: Yield curves as at 07/06/2012

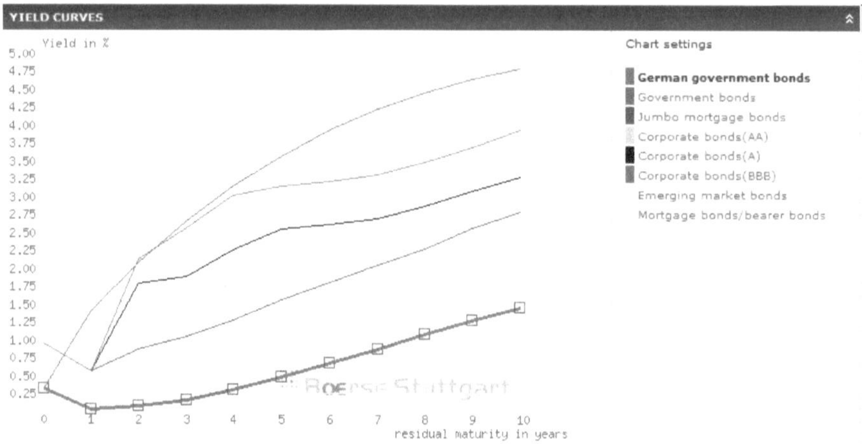

German government bonds - As at: 07/06/2012

residual maturity in years	0	1	2	3	4	5	6	7	8	9	10	>10
Yield in %	0.320	0.030	0.070	0.160	0.300	0.480	0.670	0.870	1.070	1.270	1.450	1.450

(Source: Boerse Stuttgart https://www.boerse-stuttgart.de/en/toolsandservices/yieldcurves/yieldcurves.html, as of 20.06.2012)

Ballwieser (2007) proposes the Svensson approximation as the most favorable method to determine the risk-free interest rate.[34] The "Institut der Wirtschaftsprüfer" (IDW)[35] also follows this approach.[36] The Svensson method is a continuous term structure approach that enables the estimation of spot rates for any maturity. The resulting equation for the zero-coupon yield curve is modeled using six parameters:[37]

$$y_f = b_0 + b_1 * \frac{1-exp\left(\frac{-m}{t_1}\right)}{\frac{m}{t_1}} + b_2 * \left(\frac{1-exp\left(\frac{-m}{t_1}\right)}{\frac{m}{t_1}} - \exp\left(\frac{-m}{t_1}\right)\right) + b_3 * \left(\frac{1-exp\left(\frac{-m}{t_2}\right)}{\frac{m}{t_2}} - \exp\left(\frac{-m}{t_2}\right)\right) \quad (3.3)$$

With y_f Risk-free spot rate term structure

$b_0 \dots b_3, t_1, t_2$ Vector of parameters describing the yield curve[38]

m Maturity at which the spot rate is calculated

Yield curves calculated with the Svensson method have a high degree of economic interpretation and are more consistent with the interest rate expectation theory.[39] Thus, the Svensson

[34] See Ballwieser (2007), p. 84.

[35] The IDW is a privately run organisation that serves the interests of its members who comprise both individual German Public Auditors and German Public Audit firms.

[36] See Reese and Wiese (2005), p. 3.

[37] See Svensson (1994), p. 6.

[38] These parameters are published on a daily basis by the Deutsche Bundesbank.

[39] See Shen, Huang (2011), p. 43.

method is also applied by most central banks.[40] However, even if this approach gained a lot of approval in the recent past, a bulk of international analysts still use ten-year government bonds for approximation.

3.1.2. Market risk-premium

The market risk-premium (MRP) is the difference between the expected return on a market portfolio[41] and the risk-free interest rate. Technically, it corresponds to the slope of the Security market line (SML) in the CAPM.[42] There are two main approaches to derive the MRP: First by using historical data and second by using forward-looking approaches.[43] Table 2 summarizes some studies that measure historical market risk premiums for the German market. The most influencing one is the paper of Stehle (2004). The IDW adapted the results and suggests a range of 4.5 to 5.5 per cent for business valuations.[44] Due to the currently low basic interest rate and high capital market risks, the IDW proposes a market risk premium on the upper range.[45] Stehle determines the market risk premium by subtracting the yearly return of the "Renten Performance Index" (REXP)[46] from the "Composite-DAX" (CDAX) and the DAX respectively. The REXP serves as proxy for the risk free interest rate. Depending on what method of mean (arithmetic vs. geometric) is used, the historical market risk premium differs between 5.46 and 2.66 percent (CDAX) and 6.02 and 2.76 per cent (DAX). Stehle recommends the arithmetic mean for valuations. Furthermore, he prefers the CDAX due to its higher market breath, in particular for small and medium- sized companies (SME's).[47] The questions – what method of calculating the mean should be applied, what is the Benchmark index, what is the length of the observation period and are the numbers pre- or after- tax – lead to significant differences among the studies. The application of historical data has the advantage of an intersubjective confirmability. On the other side, it is not compatible with the CAPM as "ex-ante"- model and the future-oriented DCF-valuation. Furthermore, the method to build an average over historical data remains questionable, since market risk-premiums are

---

[40] See Benkert (2004), p. 50.

[41] A market portfolio can be represented by the S&P 500, the HDAX, the DAX etc., depending on the investment horizon.

[42] See www.investopia.com, http://www.investopedia.com/terms/m/marketriskpremium.asp#axzz1xCL99zcx, as of 24.06.2012.

[43] See Damodaran (2008), p. 1.

[44] See FM-IDW 2009, S. 696f.

[45] See www.idw.de, http://www.idw.de/idw/portal/d616038/index.jsp, as of 01.06.2012.

[46] The REXP is the "Deutsche Rentenindex" as performance index. It expresses the value of a representative segment of the German bond market.

[47] See Stehle (2004), p. 921.

not constant, but change over time. Stehle suggests a deduction of 1 to 1.5 per cent from the historical mean to take the contemporary higher possibilities of diversification into account.[48]

Table 2: Historical market risk-premiums for the German market

Authors	Period	Market portfolio	Risk-free interest rate	Market risk-premium		Delta
				arithmetic	geometric	
Stehle (2004)[49]	1955 - 2003	CDAX	REXP	5.46 %	2.66 %	2.80 %
		DAX	REXP	6.02 %	2.76 %	3.26 %
Baetge/ Krause (1994)	1977 - 1991	FAZ-Index	Yield of public bonds		4.20 %	
Bimberg (1993)	1954 - 1988	Index of the "Stat. Bundesamt"	Long-term government bonds	8.20 %	5.30 %	2.90 %
			Overnight money	9.70 %	6.80 %	2.90 %

(Source: Own representation with regard to Stehle (1999), p. 19.)

The problem with a historical approach is that it is backward-looking. One possibility of a forward-looking approach is a simple dividend discount model (DDM). Within this model, the equity value can be calculated by discounting the expected future dividend payments. A second approach to achieve future-oriented risk-premiums is by linking the market risk premiums of equities to the default spread[50] of corporate bonds.[51] This approach bases on the assumption that risky securities of different asset classes should be priced consistently. Damodaran (2008) finds that the average ratio of the market risk premium to a Baa rated default spread from 1960 to 2007 is 2.41 and the median 2.02. He finds a high variation in the ratio (MRP – Baa[52] default spread) which would oppose the advantage of the approach. However, this disadvantage is compensated by a reverting median. [53] A third forward-looking approach is to ask analysts, investors, financial managers, or professors about their expectations regarding MRPs for single countries. Table 3 illustrates a survey with forecasts of financial experts for different countries in 2011. The analysts estimate significantly lower MRPs for countries like Germany, the USA, or the United Kingdom (median of 5.0 percent) than for countries

[48] See Stehle (2004), p. 921.
[49] See Stehle (2004), p. 921.
[50] The default spread of a corporate bond is the difference in yield of a risky bond in comparison to a risk-free bond, to compensate the investor for the default risk. The worse the rating, the higher is the yield.
[51] See Damodaran (2008), p. 63 f.
[52] Baa is a rating by Moody's. It stands for an investment grade bond with a relatively low risk of default.
[53] See Damodaran (2008), p. 64.

like Argentina (9.0 percent) and China (7.8 percent). Surprisingly, regarding the European debt crisis, Spain (5.5 percent) and Italy (5.0 percent) are still estimated very low.

Table 3: Market risk premiums – Analysts' and professors' forecasts for 2011

	Average	Median	St. Dev.	Q1	Q3	P10%	P90%	Max.	Min.	Number of answers
United States	**5.5**	5.0	**1.7**	4.5	6.0	4.0	7.0	15.0	1.5	1,503
Spain	**5.9**	5.5	**1.6**	5.0	6.0	4.5	8.0	15.0	1.5	930
United Kingdom	**5.3**	5.0	**2.2**	4.0	6.0	4.0	7.2	22.0	1.5	112
Italy	**5.5**	5.0	**1.4**	4.6	6.1	4.0	7.2	10.0	2.0	76
Germany	**5.4**	5.0	**1.4**	4.5	6.1	4.0	7.2	12.4	3.0	71
Mexico	**7.3**	6.4	**2.7**	5.9	9.1	5.0	10.2	16.0	1.4	56
Netherlands	**5.5**	5.0	**1.9**	4.4	6.2	3.9	7.2	12.5	2.5	48
France	**6.0**	6.0	**1.5**	5.0	7.0	4.8	7.2	11.4	2.0	45
Switzerland	**5.7**	5.5	**1.3**	5.0	6.6	4.0	7.2	9.6	3.8	44
Australia	**5.8**	5.2	**1.9**	5.0	6.0	4.0	7.1	14.0	3.0	40
Colombia	**7.5**	7.0	**4.3**	5.5	8.0	2.0	14.6	20.5	2.0	38
Sweden	**5.9**	5.5	**1.4**	5.0	7.2	4.8	7.2	10.6	3.9	38
Russia	**7.5**	6.5	**3.7**	5.5	8.0	5.0	11.0	25.0	1.3	37
Canada	**5.9**	5.0	**2.1**	5.0	6.0	4.0	8.0	14.5	3.5	36
Brazil	**7.7**	7.0	**4.6**	5.3	8.0	4.3	10.5	30.0	1.5	35
Greece	**7.4**	7.2	**2.7**	5.0	8.3	5.0	11.7	15.0	3.0	34
South Africa	**6.3**	6.0	**1.5**	5.6	6.5	5.0	7.0	11.8	4.5	34
Argentina	**9.9**	9.0	**3.4**	8.0	11.0	7.2	14.6	20.0	5.0	33
Portugal	**6.5**	6.1	**1.7**	5.0	7.2	5.0	7.2	14.0	4.5	33
Austria	**6.0**	5.7	**1.8**	5.0	7.2	4.6	7.2	14.3	3.5	32
Belgium	**6.1**	6.1	**1.0**	5.0	7.2	5.0	7.2	8.0	5.0	31
Chile	**5.7**	5.3	**2.1**	5.0	6.0	5.0	6.5	15.0	1.3	31
China	**9.4**	7.8	**5.1**	6.5	10.7	6.0	14.5	30.0	4.0	31

(Source: See Fernandez et al. (2011), p. 6.)

The question remains, which of the discussed approaches performs best? Since valuation is future-oriented, a forward-looking approach should be superior. Damodaran (2008) finds that an implied market risk premium at the end of the prior period reaches the highest correlation with the implied premium next year (0.758) and the actual risk premium the next ten years (0.376), whereas the historical premium approach performs worst.[54] Summing up, it is difficult to determine the right MRP, an implied one seems to be preferable and the MRP changes over time. These facts should be considered by analysts.

3.1.3. Beta factor

The beta factor[55] is a measure of the systematic risk that cannot be diversified. It expresses the correlation of a stock with the market portfolio. If a company is listed on a stock exchange, the beta factor can be determined using a linear regression of historical data. To obtain a valid

[54] See Damodaran (2008), p. 69 f.

[55] Stocks with a beta > 1 are riskier than the market portfolio, stocks with a beta < 1 are less risky than the market portfolio and stocks with a beta = 0 are risk-less. The beta factor includes no idiosyncratic risks like management failures or production blackouts.

result, historical data over a period of five years should be available.[56] In practice, beta factors are often regressed on a daily basis over the past one year (for example Deutsche Börse). The financial services provider Bloomberg, amongst others, delivers two year-betas on the basis of weekly returns.[57] Dörschell et al. (2008) compare the range of the beta factor of the Deutsche Bank to the DAX, applying the three calculation methods that are common in practice.[58] They find a difference of 0.224 between the "one-year /daily"- beta and the "two-year /weekly"-beta. Since the beta factor influences the cost of equity of a company, the denominator in the valuation model will be influenced.[59] As a consequence, the risk premium rises up to 1.12 per cent for the Deutsche Bank.[60] It is evident that this would have a significant impact on the valuation of the company. For valuation purposes, Dörschell et al. (2008) suggest the application of a five-year beta on a monthly basis. The two remaining approaches should be used for plausibility checks.[61]

Table 4: Determination of the Deutsche Bank beta factor using three approaches

Deutsche Bank versus Xetra Dax as at 01/08/2008	
Observation period	**Return Intervals**
5-years / monthly	1.129
2-years / weekly	1.057
1-year / daily	1.281
Range	**0.224**

(Source: Own representation based on Dörschell et al. (2008), p. 1155.)

Beside the observation period and the return interval, the beta factor can also be influenced by the so-called "day-of-the-week effect"[62], and tax-, currency-, or financing aspects.

---

[56] See Nguyen (2008), p. 193.
[57] See Dörschell et al. (2008), p. 1156.
[58] See table 4.
[59] Assume a simplified valuation model of: $V = \sum \frac{CF}{(1+r_e)^t}$ with V = Entity value of the company, CF = Cash Flows, r_e= cost of equity, and t = time. Applying the highest beta factor (1.281) in comparison to the lowest (1.057), leads to an increase in the cost of equity of 1.12 per cent in the calculation of Dörschell et al. (2008).
[60] See Dörschell et al. (2008), p. 1155.
[61] See Dörschell et al. (2008), p. 1156.
[62] The „week-of-the-day" - effect describes the influence of the day (Monday, Tuesday, Wednesday etc.) (when the beta factor regression starts) on the beta factor. Watrin et al. (2011) find that the selection of the week-day exerts a significant influence on the beta factor and the valuation of a company. See Watrin et al. (2011), p. 176.

If companies are not listed on a stock exchange, the beta factor cannot be determined using regressions of historical data. The beta factor can be calculated via a benchmark approach, instead. For this purpose, listed companies have to be identified that face a similar business risk than the target company.[63] According to Geginat et al. (2006), this should include the following five steps:[64]

1. Longlist: On the basis of wider filter criteria, a long list of comparable companies will be worked out.
2. Shortlist: Idiosyncratic filter criteria are determined, like the balance sheet, sales, financing conditions etc.
3. Peer-group: The companies of the shortlist are analyzed in detail and the best matches form the peer-group.
4. Un-levering: All peer-group beta factors are adjusted for the capital structure, i.e. hypothetical un-levered beta factors are calculated. This can be done using the Modigliani-Miller[65] formula:

   $$\beta_u = \frac{\beta_l}{1+(1-t)*\frac{D}{E}} \qquad (3.4)$$

   With β_u = unlevered beta factor, β_l = levered beta factor, t = tax rate, D = debt and E = equity. It is important to use market figures. Equity is the market capitalization. Since it is difficult to obtain a market debt value, debt can be proxied by the book debt. After calculating the unlevered betas of the peer-group, it is reasonable to use an average value (either equally-weighted, or according to subjective estimations).
5. Re-levering: The average value of the un-levered peer-group betas is plugged in the following formula to obtain the beta factor for a company which is not listed on an exchange.

   $$\beta_l = \beta_u * \left[1 + (1-t) * \frac{D}{E}\right] \qquad (3.5)$$

3.1.4. Criticism and extensions

The previous pages discussed various approaches to determine the single components (risk-free interest rate, MRP and beta factor) of the CAPM. It was shown that even small deviations in the methods of calculation, lead to significant different values. But not only the determination of the components, but also the CAPM as a comprehensive theoretical concept, faces

[63] See Nguyen (2008), p. 195.
[64] See Geginat et al. (2006), p. 23.
[65] See Modigliani and Miller (1958).

more and more criticism in the recent past. Although, the CAPM is still the main concept in use,[66] Fama and French already wrote an article in the Journal of Finance in the year 1996, with the header: "The CAPM is Wanted, Dead or Alive".[67] The problems of the CAPM mainly base on its restrictive assumptions:

- Since homogenous expectations of investors cannot be identified in practice, historical data have to be used to determine the MRP and the beta-factor. Thus, the CAPM becomes an "ex-post"-model.
- The assumptions that there are no transaction costs and no taxes, are not maintainable in practice. In addition, the idiosyncratic risk cannot be diversified completely.
- In particular, the CAPM includes no components that consider financial difficulties or insolvency risks.[68] Portfolio managers do not think in terms of variance as a measure of risk. They rather use tracking error measures.[69]
- Even Markowitz (2005) argues for more realistic assumptions. He, in particular, doubts the assumption that all investors can borrow and lend money without any limit. If this assumption would be substituted by a real-world version, the market portfolio would no longer be an efficient portfolio. Furthermore, he argues that in this situation the assumption of a representative investor could not be maintained and that the expected returns would no longer be linearly related to betas.[70]

Since the implementation of the CAPM, several empirical contradictions have been detected.[71] Banz (1981) finds that size (stock's price times shares outstanding) increases the explanatory power of the cross-section of average returns. Using only the beta factor as a proxy for risk, would overestimate the average returns for small stocks (low size) and underestimate the average returns for high stocks (high size).[72] Bhandari (1988) identifies a positive relationship between leverage and the average return.[73] This contradicts the CAPM, since the beta factor should already include leverage risk. Rosenberg et al. (1985) figure out that average stock returns are positively correlated to the ratio of a company's book value to its market value (B/P).[74] Chan et al. (1991) confirm the results of Rosenberg et al. for Japanese stocks.[75] Basu

[66] According to a study by Roland Berger, two third of the surveyed companies still work with the classical (not-adjusted) beta factor. See Geginat et al. (2006), p. 15.
[67] Fama/ French (2006), p. 1947.
[68] See Cummins / Trainar (2009), p. 471.
[69] See Montier (2009), p. 25.
[70] See Markowitz (2005), p. 27 f.
[71] A detailed discussion about the determinants that can explain stock returns will be done in section 4.
[72] See Banz (1981), p. 3.
[73] See Bhandari (1988), p. 507.
[74] See Rosenberg et al. (1985), p. 9.

(1983) demonstrates that the ratio of earnings-to-price (E/P) helps to explain the cross-section of average returns on U.S. stocks in calculations that also include size and beta.[76] Fama and French (1996) calculate the returns for 1928 – 1993 on β-deciles of NYSE[77] stocks.[78] They form ten portfolios in June of each year using betas on the NYSE value-weight market portfolio, estimated of two to five years of past monthly returns. They find that the relation between beta and the average return is rather flat,[79] that is, that high beta portfolios have no significant higher return than low beta portfolios. They come to the conclusion that beta alone does not suffice to explain expected stock returns.[80]

Table 5: Fama and French (1996) beta factor summary statistics

	Low β	2	3	4	5	6	7	8	9	High β
	Monthly Postformation Returns: 792 Months									
Mean	1.10	1.16	1.23	1.34	1.39	1.32	1.33	1.44	1.45	1.39
Std	5.12	5.76	6.30	6.99	7.66	7.98	8.31	9.50	9.84	11.10
	Annual Postformation Returns: 66 Years									
Mean	14.91	15.53	16.43	17.73	17.98	17.03	17.19	18.44	18.44	17.40
Std	25.69	26.39	28.25	29.85	29.52	30.76	32.04	35.96	36.03	40.55

(Source: See Fama / French (1996), p. 1951.)

The CAPM has been extended in a variety of forms. Some of the extensions include allowing heterogeneous beliefs; restricting the possibility of risk-free borrowing and lending; allowing a multi- time period; extensions to an international context; tax considerations;[81] and the paradigm shifting Fama-French three factor model.

3.2. Fama and French three factor model

Fama and French (1992) find that the variables market equity (price of a stock) and the ratio of book equity to market equity (B/P), as well as size (stock price times shares outstanding) explain much of the cross-section of average stock returns.[82] They argue that under the assumption of rational pricing, these variables must represent the sensitivity to common risk factors in stock returns. Fama and French (1993) use the time-series regression approach of Black, Jensen, and Scholes (1972). Monthly returns on stocks are regressed on the returns to a

[75] See Chan et al. (1991), p. 1739.
[76] See Basu (1983), p. 129.
[77] NYSE stands for New York Stock exchange.
[78] See table 5.
[79] See Fama and French (1996), p. 1952.
[80] See Fama and French (1996), p. 1947.
[81] See Brennan (1970); Wiese (2006).
[82] See Fama and French (1992), p. 427.

market portfolio and hedging portfolios for size and book-to-price ratios (B/P).[83] They find that a three-factor pricing model that includes the market factor beta and risk factors pertained to size and B/P seems to have a significant explanatory power for the cross-section of average stock returns:[84] The model states that the expected return of a portfolio $r_{pt}(t)$ in excess of the risk free rate $r_f(t)$ is explained by the sensitivity of its return to three factors: (i) the excess return on a broad market portfolio $r_m(t) - r_f(t)$, (ii) the difference between the returns on diversified portfolios of small stocks and big stocks (SMB) and (iii) the difference between the returns on diversified portfolios of high book-to-market (value) stocks and low book-to-market (growth) stocks (HML). The model is as follows:

$$r_{pt}(t) = r_f(t) + \beta_{mkt,i}\left[r_m(t) - r_f(t)\right] + \beta_{SMB,i}SMB(t) + \beta_{HML,i}HML(t) + \varepsilon_p(t) \quad (3.6)$$

With: $\beta_{mkt,i}$[85] = coefficient loading for the excess return of the market portfolio over the risk-free interest rate.

$\beta_{SMB,i}$ = coefficient loading for the excess average returns of portfolios of small stocks minus high stocks (SMB).

$\beta_{HML,i}$ = coefficient loading for the excess average returns of portfolios of high book-to-market stocks minus low book-to-market stocks (HML).

$\varepsilon_p(t)$ = error term for portfolio p at time t.

To do a historical regression analysis, a new variable α_i is introduced and the terms in the above formula are rearranged the following:

$$r_{pt}(t) - r_f(t) = \alpha_i + \beta_{mkt,i}\left[r_m(t) - r_f(t)\right] + \beta_{SMB,i}SMB(t) + \beta_{HML,i}HML(t) + \varepsilon_p(t) \quad (3.7)$$

α_i is the intercept of the regression and should be statistically indistinguishable from zero. If α_i is not equal to zero, the factors in the model cannot fully explain the portfolio returns. In the context of portfolio management, α_i indicates the relative performance of a fund manager to the market. If an investment fund generated a positive alpha, the manager outperformed the market, vice versa. Therefore, α_i can serve as a backward-looking performance measure.

The SMB and HML factors are constructed as follows: At the end of June of each year all stocks are ranked according to the median into two size portfolios, small and big (S and B).

[83] See Fama and French (1993), p. 4.
[84] See Fama and French (1993), p. 5.
[85] $\beta_{mkt,i}$ is analogous to the classical CAPM beta, but not equal, due to the additional factors SMB and HML.

Both size portfolios are then split into three BE/ME portfolios based on the quantiles 30% (low), 30% to 70% (medium), and the top 30% (high). From the intersections six portfolios (S/L, S/M, S/H, B/L, B/M, B/H) are constructed. For example B/L represents the portfolio of big sized stocks and low book-to-market stocks. The portfolios are rebalanced once a year in the beginning of July. Value-weighted returns r_t are calculated monthly for each portfolio. The factor mimicking portfolios SMB and HML can be interpreted as zero-investment portfolio, since the simultaneous long and short position requires no investment costs. SMB and HML are calculated as:[86]

$$SMB_t = \frac{\left(r_t^{\frac{S}{L}} - r_t^{\frac{B}{L}}\right) + \left(r_t^{\frac{S}{M}} - r_t^{\frac{B}{M}}\right) + \left(r_t^{\frac{S}{H}} - r_t^{\frac{B}{H}}\right)}{3} \qquad (3.8)$$

$$HML_t = \frac{\left(r_t^{\frac{S}{H}} - r_t^{\frac{S}{L}}\right) + \left(r_t^{\frac{B}{H}} - r_t^{\frac{B}{L}}\right)}{2} \qquad (3.9)$$

The factors are constructed this way in order to minimize the correlations among each other. Thus HML can be interpreted as the return of a portfolio that is long in high book-to-market stocks and short in low book-to-market stocks, and one that is widely independent from the market factor and the size effect.[87]

Fama and French (1993) investigate U.S. stock returns between 1963 and 1991. As dependent variables, they form 25 value-weighted portfolios according to size (market equity ME) and book-to-market equity (BE/ME). The portfolios generate a range of excess monthly returns from 0.32% to 1.05%.[88] The results indicate a positive relation between the BE/ME ratio and average returns and a negative relation between size and average returns. However, most of the portfolios of the two lower quintiles of the BE/ME portfolios show excess returns that are less than two standard errors from zero (t-statistics (t) < 2). This is due to the high standard deviations of the stocks that range between 4.27 and 7.76 among the different portfolios.[89]

[86] See Fama and French (1993), pp. 8 – 10.
[87] See Ammann and Steiner (2008), p. 9.
[88] See table 6.
[89] See Fama and French (1993), p. 13.

Table 6: Fama and French (1993) portfolio excess returns

Dependent variables: Excess returns on 25 stock portfolios formed on *ME* and *BE/ME*

Book-to-market equity (*BE/ME*) quintiles

Size quintile	Low	2	3	4	High	Low	2	3	4	High
	Means					Standard deviations				
Small	0.39	0.70	0.79	0.88	1.01	7.76	6.84	6.29	5.99	6.27
2	0.44	0.71	0.85	0.84	1.02	7.28	6.42	5.85	5.33	6.06
3	0.43	0.66	0.68	0.81	0.97	6.71	5.71	5.27	4.92	5.69
4	0.48	0.35	0.57	0.77	1.05	5.97	5.44	5.03	4.95	5.75
Big	0.40	0.36	0.32	0.56	0.59	4.95	4.70	4.38	4.27	4.85
	t-statistics for means									
Small	0.93	1.88	2.33	2.73	2.97					
2	1.11	2.05	2.69	2.91	3.11					
3	1.18	2.12	2.39	3.04	3.15					
4	1.49	1.19	2.08	2.88	3.36					
Big	1.50	1.42	1.34	2.43	2.26					

(Source: See Fama / French (1993), p. 15.)

Fama and French (1993) further calculate an average risk premium of the market beta (corresponds to the average value of $r_m - r_f$) of 0.43% per month (t = 1.76), an average SMB return of 0.27% per month (t = 1.73), and an average HML premium of 0.40 % per month (t = 2.91).[90] They finally find that adding the two factors SMB and HML leads to strong increases in R^2 [91]. As can be seen in table 7, only two out of 25 portfolios have a R^2 that equals to 0.90 or above. In particular, low size and high BE/ME portfolios face a low explanatory power. The three factor model creates 21 portfolios that are greater than 0.90, instead (table 7). Thus, adding the two factors SMB and HML, increases the explanatory power on average about 15.2 percent points (from 0.7792 to 0.9312).

Table 7: Fama and French (1993): Explanatory power of the market model

	R^2					$s(e)$				
Small	0.67	0.70	0.68	0.65	0.61	4.46	3.76	3.55	3.56	3.92
2	0.79	0.79	0.76	0.76	0.71	3.34	2.96	2.85	2.59	3.25
3	0.84	0.84	0.80	0.79	0.74	2.65	2.28	2.33	2.26	2.90
4	0.89	0.90	0.87	0.80	0.76	2.01	1.73	1.84	2.21	2.83
Big	0.89	0.92	0.84	0.79	0.69	1.66	1.35	1.73	1.95	2.69

(Source: See Fama and French (1993), p. 20.)

[90] See Fama and French (1993), p. 13.

[91] The coefficient of determination R^2 gives an indication of the explanatory power (goodness of fit) of a model.

Table 8: Fama and French (1993): Explanatory power of the three factor model

	R^2					$s(e)$				
Small	0.94	0.96	0.97	0.97	0.96	1.94	1.44	1.16	1.12	1.22
2	0.95	0.96	0.95	0.95	0.96	1.55	1.27	1.31	1.16	1.23
3	0.95	0.94	0.93	0.93	0.93	1.45	1.41	1.43	1.32	1.52
4	0.94	0.93	0.91	0.89	0.89	1.46	1.48	1.49	1.63	1.88
Big	0.94	0.92	0.88	0.90	0.83	1.16	1.32	1.55	1.36	2.02

(Source: See Fama and French (1993), p. 25)

Fama and French (1998) extend the three-factor model to a global context. They point out that value stocks, sorted on B/M, perform better than growth stocks in twelve out of thirteen markets between 1975 and 1995. In their calculations, global portfolios on value stocks outperform portfolios on growth stocks on average by 7.68 per cent per year (t = 3.45). They further confirm that a two-factor model, including the world market and the world B/M ratio, has a better explanatory power than an international CAPM.[92]

3.3. Explanation approaches for the value premium

The academic consensus agrees that value investing strategies, on average, outperform growth investing strategies, i.e. that there is a value premium. Challenging is the question, how this premium can be explained. Basically, there are two points of view. The first is represented by Fama and French, the second by the so called behavioralists. Fama and French take the position of the efficient market hypothesis and assign the higher returns of value investing to its increased risk.[93] The efficient market hypothesis implies that markets are very efficient in reflecting information about individual securities and the whole market. The theory further states that when new information arises, it will be immediately priced in any security. Hence, neither technical, nor fundamental analyses would help an investor to achieve excess returns in comparison to a randomly selected portfolio of individual stocks. Zhang (2005) suggests an explanation for the view that value stocks are more risky than growth stocks. He argues that because of costly reversibility and countercyclical price of risk, value firms are less flexible than growth firms to mitigate the impact of negative shocks. As a consequence, value firms face a higher risk than growth firms in recessions when the price of risk is high.[94] Gulen et al. (2008) confirm these countercyclical variations of expected stock returns by applying a Markov switching framework.[95]

---

[92] See Fama and French (1998), p. 1997.
[93] See for example Fama (1998), p. 287.
[94] See Zhang (2005), p. 95.
[95] See Gulen et al. (2008), p. 1.

The behavioralists do not believe that the value premium can be explained by the efficient market hypothesis. De Bondt and Thaler (1985) rank portfolios according to three- to five-year past returns and find that prior losers tend to outperform prior winners in the future, and vice versa. They explain their results with the overreaction hypothesis, i.e. investors consider too much the past and recent performance of stocks in their decision making process, whereas they underweight base rate data, like the fact that stock returns tend to mean-revert.[96] Lakonishok et al. (1994) suggest that the value strategies perform better than growth strategies, since they exploit the irrational behavior of investors.[97] Consistent with the empirical evidence, they find an annually value premium of 10 to 11 percent. They suggest that their results can be best explained by the preference of investors for growth strategies. Since the high expectations, that are reflected in these stocks, are often not fulfilled, value strategies perform better than growth strategies.[98] Beside the existence of the value premium, its persistence over a long time period has been discussed extensively. Basically, every anomaly is expected to be arbitraged after its detection. Behavioral aspects may explain several impediments in arbitrage.[99]

An additional explanation for the value premium is proposed by Kothari et al. (1995). They find that the higher returns of value strategies would be due to data selection biases.[100] However, Chan et al. (1995) oppose this explanation. They point out that there is no severe selection bias on the database "Compustat".[101]

3.4. Carhart four factor model

Carhart (1997) extends the three-factor model of Fama and French by adding a momentum factor. The model can then be written as:

$$r_{pt}(t) - r_f(t) = \alpha_i + \beta_{mkt,i}\left[r_m(t) - r_f(t)\right] + \beta_{SMB,i}SMB(t) + \beta_{HML,i}HML(t) + \beta_{UMD,i}UMD(t) + \varepsilon_p(t) \qquad (3.10)$$

$UMD(t)$ captures Jegadeesh and Titman's (1993)[102] one-year momentum anomaly and is long in last year's short-term winners and short in last year's short-term losers. $\beta_{UMD,i}$ is the corre-

[96] See De Bondt and Thaler (1985), p. 793.
[97] See Lakonishok et al. (1994), p. 1541.
[98] See Lakonishok et al. (1994), p. 1576 f.
[99] See Shleifer / Vishny (1997), p. 54.
[100] See Kothari et al. (1995), p. 221.
[101] See Chan et al. (1995), p. 292.
[102] See Jegadeesh and Titman (1993), p. 65 – 91.

sponding factor loading. The momentum is the cumulative return from month $\tau - 12$ to $\tau - 2$. The most recent month is not considered, to avoid the short-term reversal effect documented by Jegadeesh and Titman (1993).[103] The UMD factor is calculated analogous to the HML factor of Fama and French (1993). According to its past year performance stocks are sorted on the 30% and 70% quantile breakpoints into portfolios of losers (D), portfolios of neutrals (N), and portfolios of winners (U). These three portfolios are again intersected with the two portfolios ranked according to size, which results in six portfolios (S/U, S/N, S/D, B/U, B/N, and B/D). UMD is then the equal-weighted return of the winner portfolios minus the loser portfolios:

$$UMD_t = \frac{\left(r_t^{\frac{S}{U}} - r_t^{\frac{S}{D}}\right) + \left(r_t^{\frac{B}{U}} - r_t^{\frac{B}{D}}\right)}{2} \qquad (3.11)$$

Carhart explains short-term persistence in equity mutual fund returns with common components in stock returns and investment costs. According to his study, a long position in last year's top-decile mutual funds and a short position in last year's worst-decile mutual funds generate an average yearly return of eight per cent. 4.6 per cent of this spread could be explained by differences in the market value and momentum, 0.7 per cent by differences in expense ratios, and one per cent by transaction costs.[104] He finds that the four-factor model does a better job in avoiding average pricing errors in comparison to the CAPM and the three-factor model of Fama and French.[105] He concludes with three rules-of-thumb for mutual fund investors. First, funds with durable poor performance should be avoided. Second, funds that performed well in the previous year, have higher returns in the next year, but not in later years. And third, the total expense ratio and transaction costs directly influence the performance.[106] Since the study of Carhart, the four-factor model has become one of the most prominent asset pricing models and its explanatory power has been confirmed in several empirical papers.[107]

[103] See Jegadeesh and Titman (1993), p. 89.
[104] See Carhart (1997), p. 79 f.
[105] See Carhart (1997), p. 62.
[106] See Carhart (1997), p. 80 f.
[107] See Daniel et al. (1997), pp.1035 – 1058; Eberhart et al. (2004), pp. 623 – 650.

4. Determinants of expected stock returns

After discussing the most important models to value stock returns, this chapter describes the potential determinants in detail. As has been demonstrated, the CAPM does a poor job in explaining stock market returns. Ever since its publication, a bulk of empirical studies has attempted to identify additional components. Assuming a rational investor, capital market anomalies would be expected to disappear after their detection due to arbitrage. However, there seem to be some anomalies with a continuous persistence. Table 9 indicates the expected direction of the different firm characteristics with the stock returns based on empirical evidence. Literature proposes that the higher the P/B and the P/E ratio, the lower is the expected stock return. Thus, a negative relationship is expected. In contrast, the dividend yield should have a positive relation with expected stock returns. The direction of the size characteristic is set in brackets due to recent findings of a reversal of the size effect.

Table 9: Components of stock returns	**Expected direction**	
	positive	**negative**
Value premium determinants		
Price-to-book (P/B) (4.1)		x
Price-earnings (P/E) (4.2)		x
Dividend yield (D/P) (4.3)	x	
Size and momentum		
Size (4.4)		(x)
Momentum (4.5)	x	
Further determinants(4.6)		

4.1. Price-to-book

$$\frac{P}{B} = \frac{\text{Market capitalization}}{\text{Book value}} = \frac{\text{Market equity}}{\text{Book equity}} = \frac{\text{Share price}}{\text{Book value per share}} \left(= \text{inverse of } \frac{B}{M} \text{ or } \frac{BE}{ME}\right)$$

The price-to-book ratio (P/B) is used to compare a company's current market price to its book price. The ratio can be useful for identifying value stocks, since it indicates whether a firm's asset value is comparable to its share price. The validity differs among industries.

It is above all useful when valuing companies that are composed of mostly liquid assets, like insurance companies or banks. The price-to-book ratio is not as useful for companies with high research- and development expenditures (R&D) or firms with high levels of property or other fixed assets. Since long-term assets are held on the balance sheet at the original cost, book values can differ strongly from market values, if market prices change.

The P/B ratio is one of the most discussed determinants in finance literature. Already Stattman (1980) finds a negative relationship between the P/B figure and the cross-section of expected stock returns,[108] i.e., higher P/B measures indicate a lower expected return than lower P/B ratios (value premium or HML). Fama and French (1992) report that the average monthly returns rise from 0.30 per cent for the highest P/B portfolio to 1.83 per cent for the lowest portfolio. This difference of 1.53 per cent is twice as high as the difference between portfolios that are ranked relating to size.[109] They further argue that the combination of P/B and size absorbs the explanatory power of the P/E ratio and leverage.[110] Fama and French (1998) find value premiums in almost all countries around the world[111], which they confirm in later studies[112]. There are few studies which neglect the influence of the P/B measure. For example, Kothari et al. (1995) find that P/B is only weakly related to average stock returns.[113]

4.2. Price-to-earnings

$$\frac{P}{E} = \frac{\text{Share price}}{\text{Earnings per share (EPS)}} = \frac{\text{Market capitalization}^{114}}{\text{net income}} \; (= \text{reciprocal of earnings yield } \frac{E}{P})$$

The P/E ratio is a method to compare a firm's current share price to its earnings per share. It can be interpreted as the unit of net income that investors are paying for a share. Thus, it can be seen as the number of years that a company had to cumulate earnings, in order to justify the purchase price. Similar to the P/B ratio, P/E ranges that are considered to be priced fairly, differ among industries. Hence, the P/E ratio can be used to evaluate certain sectors or to compare the prices of companies within the same sector. In order to account for differences in growth, the P/E ratio can be adjusted by the expected growth in EPS and becomes to the price- earnings-growth ratio (PEG) (PEG = $\frac{P/E}{g}$ with g = growth rate).

Empirical research starts with Ball (1978). He points out that the P/E ratio can be seen as a direct proxy for expected stock returns.[115] Basu (1983) argues that stocks of low P/E firms

108 See Stattman (1980), p. 25.
109 See Fama and French (1992), p. 441.
110 See Fama and French (1992), p. 445.
111 See Fama and French (1998), p. 1997.
112 See for example Fama and French (2010), p. 22 f.
113 See Kothari et al. (1995), p. 186.
114 Market capitalization/net income corresponds to the P/E ratio, only if there was no change in the number of outstanding shares during the observed periods (market capitalization = price times current number of shares, whereas earnings per share = net income/weighted average number of shares).

generate significant higher risk-adjusted returns than stocks of high P/E firms.[116] Fama and French (1992) find that the P/E determinant loses its explanatory power , when the regression consists of the beta factor, size and the P/B.[117] In contrast, Artmann et al. (2011) figure out that the value effect is not only captured by the P/B, but also by the P/E ratio. They find that a four factor model that consists of beta, P/B, P/E, and momentum does the best job in explaining German stock returns.[118]

Studies on the PEG ratio are limited. Peters (1991) finds that within the period 1982 till1989, USD 1 invested in the lowest PEG portfolio would have turned to USD 15.36, whereas the highest PEG portfolio would have turned only to USD 1.38.[119] Easton (2004) develops a model of earnings and earnings growth and compares the results with the estimates implied by the P/E and PEG ratio. He finds that the results implied by the PEG ratio have a higher correlation to his model and a lower downward-sloping bias than the results implied by the P/E ratio.[120]

4.3. Dividend yield

$$\frac{D}{P} = \frac{\text{Most recent annual dividend per share}}{\text{share price}} = \frac{\text{Total dividends}}{\text{market capitalization}} \left(= \text{reciprocal of } \frac{P}{D}\right)$$

The dividend yield can be interpreted as the return in per cent that an investor receives via dividends in relation to the current share price. There is an inverse relationship between the yield and the stock price. If the share price doubles, the dividend yield will be the half, and vice versa. It is not mandatory for companies to pay dividends. In particular, growth firms often only pay low or no dividends, since they retain earnings to invest in future growth. Stock markets react very fast on companies' announcements to change their dividend policy. Historically, many investors preferred companies that paid high dividend yields, since these imply an underpriced stock and a higher stability. The discussion of the influence of the dividend yield on stock returns has a long history in scientific papers.

Whereas Black and Scholes (1973) find no difference in expected returns of high yield and low yield stocks,[121] Fama and French (1988) point out that regressions of returns related to dividend yields have an explanatory power, in particular, when considering longer return ho-

---

[115] See Ball (1978), p. 103.
[116] See Basu (1983), p. 129.
[117] See Fama and French (1992), p. 445.
[118] See Artmann et al. (2011), p. 20.
[119] See Peters (1991), p. 49.
[120] See Easton (2004), p. 73.
[121] See Black and Scholes (1974), p. 1.

rizons.[122] The results of Naranjo et al. (1998) suggest a strong positive relation between the dividend yield and the expected stock returns, even after applying the Fama/French three-factor model. They further argue that the effect would be larger for small size companies.[123] Kothari and Shanken (1997) also support evidence that the dividend yield tracks variation in expected stock returns between 1926 and 1991. In the sub-period 1941 – 1991, they find that the D/P effect is stronger than the P/B effect.[124]

4.4. Size

$$\text{Size} = \text{Market capitalization} = \text{Market equity (ME, M)} = \text{share price} * \text{number of shares}$$

Market capitalization or size represents the total value of a company's shares and thus, the public consensus on its equity value. Traditionally, companies are classified in large-, mid-, and small- caps. Large-caps face a market capitalization greater than EUR 2 bn, mid-caps are between EUR 500 m and EUR 2 bn, and small-caps below EUR 500 m. However, there is no uniform definition about the cutoffs. Beside the turnover of traded shares, the market capitalization is a crucial criterion regarding the admittance of the stock in a certain index.

Whereas, earlier studies usually find evidence for a size premium[125], current works often negate any significant impact. Banz (1981) points out that smaller firms had higher risk-adjusted returns than larger firms.[126] Fama and French (1992) also figure out a significant size premium and use size in combination with beta and the P/B ratio for their extension of the CAPM. There are many other studies that identify a size effect.[127] In contrast, Dimson and Marsh (1999) find evidence that the size premium reversed in the United Kingdom (U.K.) in the 1990s.[128] Horowitz et al. (2000) investigate the relationship between expected returns and the size effect between 1980 and 1996 and find no size premium.[129] Artmann et al. (2011) detect a negative, but statistically insignificant size premium for the German market.[130]

---

[122] See Fama and French (1988), p. 4.
[123] See Naranjo et al. (1998), p. 2031.
[124] See Kothari and Shanken (1997), p. 169.
[125] The size premium is a stock market anomaly that states that small companies on average perform better than large companies.
[126] See Banz (1981), p. 3.
[127] See, for example, Rouwenhorst (1999); Barber and Lyon (1997).
[128] See Dimson and Marsh (1999), p. 53.
[129] Horowitz et al. (2000), p. 143.
[130] See Artmann et al. (2011), p. 20.

4.5. Momentum

Momentum = Cumulative past return of a stock over a certain time period

The implementation of momentum is an investment strategy that aims to generate profit on the continuance of trends in the market. Momentum investors believe that stocks that had a large price increase will continue to have additional gains, and vice versa. To execute this strategy, a trader will take a long position in stocks that show an upward trending price and short sell stocks with a downward trend.

Momentum is no fundamental, but a technical firm characteristic that is based on the technical chart analysis. Figure 3 shows the share price development of the Adidas stock within the past one year and the related momentum indicator. The momentum is measured within a 12-days period and can be interpreted in percent.[131] A momentum above the 100 per cent line indicates an upward-sloping trend, and vice versa. Some investors even consider the breakthrough of the line to be a buy- or sell- signal.

Figure 3: Momentum of the Adidas stock

(Source: www.onvista.de)

The momentum effect is one of the most puzzling asset pricing anomalies. Jegadeesh and Titman (1993) document that momentum strategies generate significant returns over horizons

[131] $Momentum = \left(\frac{Closing\ price\ today\ (t)}{Closing\ price\ (t-12)}\right) * 100.$

of 3 - 12 months during the 1965 – 1989 period.[132] They report that a strategy that groups stocks related to their past six-months returns and hold these stocks for six months, generates an excess average return of 12.01 per cent per year.[133] They further state that the hedge portfolios (winner minus loser portfolios) realized positive returns in each of the 12 months after the formation date, with the exception of the first month.[134] Rouwenhorst (1998) finds that an internationally diversified portfolio of past winners outperforms a portfolio of past loser by about one per cent per month.[135]And as already mentioned earlier, Carhart (1997) extended the Fama/French three-factor model among a momentum factor.

4.6. Further determinants

Some studies examine additional value premium proxies like a price-to-cash-flow ratio (P/CF)[136], a price-to-sales ratio (P/S)[137], or a debt-to-equity ratio (D/E = leverage)[138]. Barbee et al. (1996) find that the P/S and the D/E ratio had a greater explanatory power than the P/B ratio and the size of company during the 1979 to 1991 period.[139] Another discussed determinant is illiquidity. Amihud (2002) introduces an illiquidity ratio which is calculated as the ratio of a stock's daily return divided by its daily dollar volume. The measure shows the impact on the stock price per unit of trading volume. He finds that the illiquidity ratio had a positive effect on expected stock returns. This was consistent with the size effect, which can be seen as another proxy for illiquidity. He further argues that the market risk premium $(r_m - r_f)$ would cover a premium for illiquidity.[140] Pastor (2003) finds that stocks that have a high sensitivity to liquidity outperform stocks that have a low sensitivity to liquidity by 7.5 per cent per year between 1966 and 1999.[141]

Another bulk of empirical research investigates the influence of macroeconomic factors on expected stock returns. Macroeconomic factors are not always covered by the systematic risk premium beta, since changes in the macro environment simultaneously affect many companies' financial figures.[142] Geske and Roll (1983) point out that both, expected and unexpected

[132] See Jegadeesh and Titman (1993), p. 65.
[133] See Jegadeesh and Titman (1993), p. 89.
[134] See above
[135] See Rouwenhorst (1998), p. 283.
[136] See for example Davis (1994), pp. 1579 - 1593.
[137] See for example Sheu et al. (1998), pp. 1 – 18.
[138] See for example Bhandari (1988), pp. 507 -528.
[139] See Barbee et al. (1996), p. 56.
[140] See Amihud (2002), p. 52 f.
[141] See Pastor (2003), p. 642.
[142] See Flannery and Protopapadakis (2002), p. 751.

inflation had a negative relation to stock returns.[143] Flannery and Protopapadakis (2002) identify six macro variables that can be seen as risk factors: two inflation measures (producer price index [PPI] and consumer price index [CPI]), three real factors (balance of trade, employment/unemployment, and housing starts), and a monetary measure (money supply M1).[144]

5. Empirical studies for the German stock market

Griffin (2002) and Fama and French (2010) show that global models do a worse job in explaining cross-sectional returns than local models. Therefore, it seems to be beneficial to discuss studies for the German market.

Heston et al. (1999) and Stehle (1997) investigate only the size effect. Heston et al. (1999) examine the influence of beta and size in explaining expected stock market returns using a sample of 12 European countries between 1978 and 1995. They find an average monthly insignificant SMB premium for Germany of 0.11 percent.[145] In contrast, Stehle (1997) reveals evidence for the size effect.[146] Fama and French (1998) investigate whether there is a value premium for countries around the world using data between 1975 and 1995. For Germany they calculate a yearly HML premium of 2.75 percent that is only slightly indifferent from zero ($t = 0.92$).[147] Schulz and Stehle (2002) find a significant HML effect, but no significant influence of the size variable. However, they argue that adding the size variable would considerable improve the explanatory power of the model.[148]

Schiereck et al. (1999) test momentum and contrarian strategies for stocks listed on the Frankfurt stock exchange between 1961 and 1991. They find that both momentum and contrarian strategies significantly beat the market index. They state that the results observed on the German market would be closely related to the findings for the U.S.[149] Koch (2010) investigates the influence of illiquidity on the cross-section of German stocks applying a different set of illiquidity proxies. After controlling for other firm characteristics, he finds a significant positive influence on stock returns. Following up the question whether size proxies for illiquidity,

---

[143] See Geske and Roll (1983), p. 1.
[144] See Flannery and Protopapadakis (2002), p. 774.
[145] See Heston et al. (1999), p. 23.
[146] See Stehle (1997), p. 237.
[147] See Fama and French (1998), p. 1980.
[148] See Schulz and Stehle (2002), p. 22.
[149] See Schiereck et al. (1999), p. 114.

he states that the two factors would be highly correlated, but could not be seen as perfect substitutes. Furthermore, he finds an insignificant negative size effect.[150]

Ziegler et al. (2007) use the methodology of Fama and French (1993) in order to explain stock market returns for the German market. They find that a three-factor model containing the market excess return, HML, and SMB does a better job than the standard CAPM. They further evaluate the explanatory power of a five-factor model that adds two characteristics from the bond markets (the term structure and a default risk component) and find no improvement.[151] They find an arithmetic monthly mean for the HML factor of 0.402 percent which is significant at the one-percent level. In contrast, the SMB factor is insignificant at 0.083 percent.[152] Hanauer et al. also apply the Fama and French (1993) methodology to examine the returns of CDAX companies between 1996 and 2011. They find an insignificant positive market risk premium of 0.554 percent, a significant positive value premium based on B/M of 0.735 percent, a significant positive momentum of 1.187 percent, and a significant negative size premium of -0.705 percent.[153] Artmann et al. (2011) investigate the German stock market in the period 1963 to 2006). They apply two technical firm characteristics (stock momentum and stock reversal) and a number of fundamental firm characteristics (size, beta, E/P, B/M, market leverage, book leverage, return on assets, and asset growth).[154] Their main finding is that a four-factor model that contains the beta-, the B/M-, the E/P-, and the momentum factor has a higher explanatory power than the Fama and French three-factor model and the Carhart four-factor model. They explain the adding of E/P with the possibility that earnings contain more information in Germany due to specific accounting standards. Like Koch (2010), they find a negative size effect in recent years.[155]

---

[150] See Koch (2010), pp. 32 – 35.
[151] See Ziegler et al. (2007), p. 34.
[152] See Ziegler et al. (2007), p. 13.
[153] See Hanauer et al. (2012), p. 14.
[154] See Artmann et al. (2011), p. 7.
[155] See Artmann et al. (2011), p. 20.

6. Own empirical analysis

6.1. Data and methodology

The sample consists of German stocks that are listed at the Frankfurt Stock Exchange between 1992 and 2011. The database used is Thomson Datastream. I do not exclude financial firms like many empirical studies suggest. Fama and French (1992), for example, exclude financial firms by arguing that these companies have a common level of leverage ratio that would indicate bankruptcy for nonfinancial firms. Thus, high leverage has to be interpreted differently among financial and nonfinancial companies.[156] Stehle (2002) also excludes financial firms, due to different valuations and accounting standards in comparison to nonfinancial firms.[157] In contrast, Barber and Lyon (1997) find no significant difference in the relation of firm characteristics and stock returns for financial and nonfinancial companies.[158] To prohibit survivorship bias, I also include companies that went bankrupt during 1992 and 2011. Thus, the number of companies in the sample changes over time due to new listings and delistings. With its insolvency, firms are excluded from the sample. Survivorship bias denotes the tendency that bankrupt companies are excluded from performance studies. As a consequence, average returns could be upward biased. Breen and Korajczyk (1993), for example, document that more than half of the P/B effect in Fama and French (1992) is due to survivorship bias.[159] The overall sample consists of 1759 stocks. In a first step, companies which do not have data for all investigated determinants are removed. By doing so, the sample is reduced to 1036 stocks. Stocks are only included in year t, if stock prices in year t-1 are available.[160] In addition, stocks with negative P/B and P/E ratios are eliminated. The P/B determinant is below zero, if a company has a negative book value of equity. Whereas, Chan et al. (1991) place negative P/Bs in a subgroup 0,[161] Lyon and Barber (1999) exclude negative P/Bs.[162] The number of firms excluded was not higher than five percent. Similarly, negative P/Es were removed, since they would imply a misleading interpretation.[163] Negative PE's were the main reason for the reduction of the sample. I also exclude penny stocks from the beginning of 2002, since the number of stocks that are priced lower than EUR 1 has increased significantly in the aftermath

156 See Fama and French (1992), p. 429.
157 See Stehle (2002), p. 13 f.
158 See Barber and Lyon (1997), p. 875.
159 See Breen and Korajczyk (1993), p. 23.
160 This is necessary to calculate the momentum of a stock.
161 See Chan et al. (1991), p. 1744.
162 See Lyon et al. (1999), p. 168.
163 Since P/E can be seen as an additional proxy for risk, high P/Es suggest higher risk. Thus, negative P/Es would imply no or low risk, which makes neither sense in a theoretical context, nor in an empirical one. Chan et al. (1991), for example, find that stocks with negative P/Es achieve a higher average return than most of the portfolios of positive P/E stocks. See Chan et al. (1991), p. 1747.

of the burst of the dot-com bubble. Penny-stocks usually face a low liquidity and even small trades can influence the share price excessively. Thus, average returns would be biased. I do not exclude any outliers, since this seems to be arbitrary and not practice-oriented in my view. Fama and French (1992), for example, remove outliers by setting them equal to the 0.005 and 0.995 fractiles. Table 10 documents the average number of firms for different years.

Table 10: Average number of firms

Year	Average number of firms	Year	Average number of firms
1992	219	2002	406
1993	218	2003	333
1994	224	2004	352
1995	239	2005	403
1996	253	2006	451
1997	280	2007	505
1998	313	2008	536
1999	351	2009	434
2000	421	2010	408
2001	455	2011	480

(Source: Data from Thomson Reuters Datastream)

As can be seen, the average number of firms increased strongly between 1996 and 2001. This is due to the "new economy boom" and the attended rise of initial public offerings (IPO's). After the burst of the "dot-com bubble" in 2000, the number of insolvencies rose with a certain time-lag. Furthermore, many companies generated negative earnings and became penny-stocks. After 2002, about 50 penny stocks were removed every month. With the recovery of the financial markets, the number of firms increased again and peaked in 2008. The sharp decline in 2009 and 2010 can be traced back to the start of the financial crisis in the mid of 2008.

I use monthly data of stocks from Thomson Reuters Datastream. The database query is done for every 15th day of a month, instead of month's end data. Thus, the problem of different month lengths can be avoided. January returns are therefore calculated from 15th December to 15th January on portfolios that are ranked in December, February returns from 15th January to 15th February, and so on. Following formula is applied:

$$r_{i,\tau} = \left(\frac{P_{i,\tau} + \frac{1}{12} * DPS_{i,\tau}}{P_{i,\tau-1}} - 1\right) * 100^{164} \qquad (6.1)$$

With $r_{i,\tau}$ = Return of stock i in month τ

$P_{i,\tau}$ = Share price of stock i in month τ

$P_{i,\tau-1}$ = Share price of stock i in month $\tau - 1$

$DPS_{i,\tau}$ = Dividend per share in month τ

The challenges on the implementation of an appropriate risk-free interest rate were discussed in 3.1.1. For the purpose of calculating monthly returns, a basic interest rate with a maturity of one month has to be identified. U.S. studies commonly apply the yield of a one-month treasury bill.[165] In their study for the German market, Artmann et al. (2011) use the one-month money market rate reported by the Deutsche Bundesbank.[166] I use the German one-month offered rate (Datastream code: FIBOR1M).[167] Since the one-month risk-free interest rate represents the annually yield, it has to be calculated on a yield per month basis:

$$r_{f,i,\tau} = \left(\sqrt[12]{1 + \frac{r_{f,1,t}}{100}} - 1\right) * 100 \qquad (6.2)$$

With $r_{f,i,\tau}$ is the yield per month of the one-month risk-free interest rate and $r_{f,1,t}$ is the yield per year for the one-month risk-free interest rate.

---

[164] This formula is not totally exact, since it neglects the reinvestment chance of DPS. The deviation, however, is marginal. A better approximation would be the following: $r_{i,\tau} = \left(\frac{P_{i,\tau}}{P_{i,\tau-1}} - 1\right) * 100 + (\sqrt[12]{1 + DY_{i,\tau}} - 1)$ with $DY_{i,\tau}$ = Dividend yield of stock i in month τ.

[165] See, for example, Fama and French (1998), p. 1982.

[166] See Artmann et al. (2011), p. 8.

[167] I compared the yields with the data published by the Deutsche Bundesbank, and found only marginal differences.

Figure 4 illustrates the development of the basic one month interest rate.

Figure 4: Germany Interbank 1 month Offered rate - yield in [%]

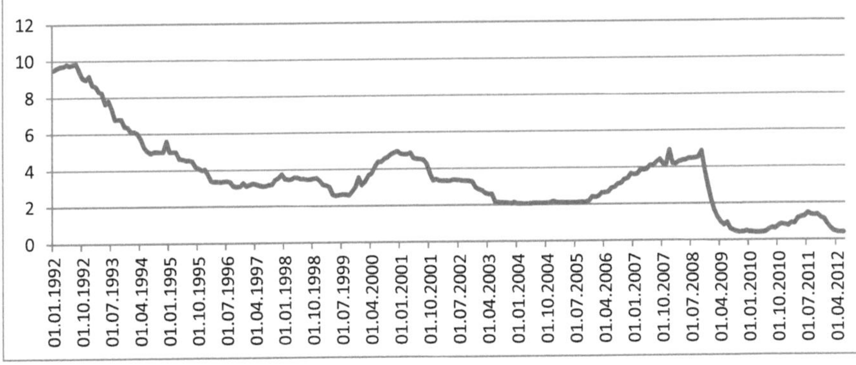

(Source: Own representation, data from Thomson Datastream)

The equity risk premium r_m is proxied by the monthly returns of the CDAX Performance Index (Datastream Code: CDAXGEN) The CDAX Performance Index includes the shares of all domestic companies listed in Prime Standard and General Standard. The index represents the whole German equity market, i.e. all companies listed on the Frankfurt Stock Exchange. The CDAX was established in December 1987 and has a base level of 100.

To explain stock market returns, I investigate the most discussed firm characteristics in the empirical asset pricing literature - three value determinants (P/B, P/E, DY), as well as size and momentum. The momentum is the cumulative return from month $\tau - 12$ to $\tau - 2$. The most recent month is not considered, to avoid the short-term reversal effect.[168] The momentum in percent is calculated as follows:

$$Momentum = \left(\frac{P_{i,\tau-2} + \frac{1}{12} * \sum_{\tau-12}^{\tau-2} DPS_i}{P_{i,\tau-12}} - 1 \right) * 100 \qquad (6.3)$$ [169]

P/B (Code: PTBV), P/E (Code: PE), DY (Code: DY), and Size (Code: MV) are retrieved from Thomson Reuters Datastream.

Basically, there are two main approaches to conduct asset pricing tests – the application of single observations versus portfolio data. The formation of portfolios reveals several ad-

---

[168] See Jegadeesh and Titman (1993), p. 89

[169] Similar to the calculation of the stock returns, this formula considers no DPS reinvestment. The modified formula would then be: $Momentum = \left(\frac{P_{i,\tau-2}}{P_{i,\tau-12}} - 1 \right) * 100 + \sum_{\tau-12}^{\tau-2} \left(\sqrt[12]{1 + DY_i} - 1 \right)$.

vantages. Since time series regressions require data for an observed company over the whole time period, many companies have to be eliminated from the sample. Through the formation of portfolios, even companies can be considered that were only listed for a certain time period. Thus, an ex-post selection bias can be avoided.[170] A further advantage of the portfolio creation is that returns of portfolios have more stable firm characteristics in comparison to single data. Hence, the assumption of the normal probability distribution is rather fulfilled.[171] As a disadvantage, the formation of portfolios is associated with a loss of information, since the estimation loses its power to consider the variance of the explanatory variables within the single portfolio. Only the variance between different portfolios remains allegeable.[172] Furthermore, all significant explanatory variables should be considered in sorting the portfolio to allow a sufficient variation.[173] This can be done by sorting sub-portfolios, "sub-sub-portfolios" and so on. However, by doing so, the number of portfolios rises exponentially and the number of stocks per portfolio converges to zero. Therefore, there is a trade-off between a high variation between the portfolios and a high number of stocks which is beneficial for diversification.[174]

Chan et al. (1991), for example, apply a threefold grouping procedure. First, they group firms into quartiles related to earnings yield (E/P). Each earnings yield group is further divided into four sub-groups ranked to size, and these sub-groups are finally divided into four B/M groups. Thus, they obtain 64 groups (4x4x4).[175] Many studies, especially relevant for the German market, employ a pairs sorting scheme. Artmann et al. (2011), for example, construct double-sorted portfolios. They rank one firm characteristic into quartiles and subdivide these into four groups of another firm characteristic. Thus, they have 16 portfolios for each characteristics pair.[176]

I deviate from the common portfolio formation procedure, in that sense, that I only construct portfolios and no sub-portfolios, since the number of stocks in the sample is comparatively low. Applying the sorting scheme from Chan et al. (1991), would lead to only three stocks per portfolio in 1992, which is far too low to be representative. Thus, a low variation between the firm characteristics will be accepted for the sake of representative portfolios. This is done by forming five portfolios based on the quintile breakpoints for each firm characteristic and cal-

---

[170] See Stehle (2002), p. 5.
[171] See Stehle (2002), p. 6.
[172] See above
[173] See Berk (2000), p. 407.
[174] See Stehle (2002), p. 7.
[175] See Chan et al. (1991), p. 1744.
[176] See Artmann et al. (2011), p. 29.

culating the hedge portfolios (portfolio five minus portfolio one). The hedge portfolio for P/B is long in low P/B's and short in high P/B's (corresponds to the HML factor of Fama and French), the hedge portfolio for P/E is long in low P/E's and short in high P/E's, the hedge portfolio for DY is long in high DY's and short in low DY's, the hedge portfolio for size is long in large firms and short in small firms (BMS = reciprocal to SMB from Fama and French), and the hedge portfolio for momentum is long in high momentum and short in low momentum (UMD). Hence, it will be investigated, whether the German market reveals still a value premium (low P/B, P/E, and high DY perform on average better than high P/B, P/E and low DY), whether high momentum portfolios achieve better returns than low momentum portfolios (UMD), and whether the reversed size effect (BMS) that was suggested by recent studies[177] is also true for German stocks.

The returns of portfolios are calculated using an equal-weighted[178] approach. This assumes that an investor purchases all stocks in a portfolio for the same absolute value. In practice, such a method would cause high transaction costs, since the portfolios would have to be rebalanced after every price change. In contrast, a value-weighting approach factors in the size of a company. As a consequence, a price change of a large company will stronger influence the portfolio return than a shift in price of a small company. However, an equal-weighted approach is preferable in capturing the cross-section of stock returns.[179]

My analysis deviates further from most of the empirical papers in that sense that I rebalance each portfolio on a monthly basis. Most studies do this once a year. Chan et al. (1991) updates each portfolio formation every year in June.[180] The same is true for Fama and French (1993).[181] They argue that fundamental firm data like the equity book value, dividends, and earnings are published only once a year in the course of the financial statement announcements. However, the ratios P/B, P/E, DY, as well as size and momentum change permanently due to continuous share price changes. Thus, if the price of a company rises excessively in a short time period, a stock can move from a value portfolio to a growth portfolio, and vice versa.

---

[177] See Dimson and Marsh (1999), p. 53.

[178] Equal-weighted portfolios are applied,for example, by Lakonishok et al. (1994), and Fama and French (1996).

[179] See Artmann et al. (2011), p. 9.

[180] See Chan et al. (1744).

[181] See Fama and French (1993), p. 11.

6.2. Descriptive statistics

Table 11 shows the summary statistics of the investigated firm characteristics P/B, P/E, DY, Size and Momentum per year. Over the whole time period, companies have a mean P/B ratio of 2.976 at a median of 1.877[182] and a standard deviation (std.dev.) of 8.008. The high difference between mean and median and the high standard deviation indicate that the values are strongly skewed by outliers. This is above all true for the year 1997, where the company "Sachsenmilch" is valued at a P/B between 669.27 and 844.32. If years with strong outliers are excluded, the average std.dev. ranges between 1.69 and 6.08. Due to the named reasons, it is preferable to consider the median in evaluating trends. Figure 4: Panel A displays the development of the P/B ratio over the sample period. Whereas the median was above 2 from 1992 to 2000, the ratio has decreased afterwards to its lowest value of 1.349 in 2009. It seems that a continuous de-rating[183] process has been taken place. A reason for this could be that the excessive earnings expectations in the course of the "new-economy boom" have been revised. However, surprisingly is the fact that the median P/B in 2000 was not substantially higher than in 1992.

Looking at the P/E ratio, outliers are responsible for even higher deviations. The mean P/E is 75.151 at a median of 19.046 and a volatility of 688.152. In the year 2000, the company "Cleanventure" trades at a P/E between 37,141 and 264,037. This means that the company would have to cumulate earnings for 264,037 years to justify its high valuation, which is obviously absurd. Two facts matter: First, some companies have been valued excessively in the course of the "new-economy boom", and more important second, the P/E ratio loses its validity, if earnings converge to zero. As can be seen in figure 4: Panel B, the P/E median runs in waves which is very similar to the P/B curve.[184]

The DY has a mean of 2.379 over the sample period, i.e. the average company pays dividends that yield 2.379 percent per year. Since the median with 1.872 (std.dev. of 3.675) is relatively close to the mean, there seem to be no substantial outliers in the sample. The median is smaller than the mean, since one fourth to one half of the companies in the sample regularly pay no dividends. The mean dividend yield is relatively constant at 2 to 3 percent until 2003, decreases to 1.77 percent in 2007, and reaches its highest value in 2009 with 3.68 percent. As

[182] This value is almost identical to the study of Artmann et al. (2011) who calculate a P/B median of 1.842 between 1962 and 2005. See Artmann et al. (2011), p. 26.

[183] A de-rating is what happens when share prices change because investors are not willing anymore to buy shares at the current valuation level.

[184] The Pearson correlation coefficient between the P/B median and the P/E median, measured on yearly average data, is 0.898.

value premium proxy, the dividend yield should be negatively[185] correlated with the two value proxies P/B and P/E. However, the correlation is close to zero.[186]

Since the sample contains many small caps, the mean of size is considerably higher than the median. Whereas the mean market-cap per company over the whole sample period exceeds EUR 1.9 billion, the median is only about EUR 150 million. What is surprising, is the fact that the mean size per company has almost doubled during the investigation period, whereas the median has nearly halved. One reason is certainly the strong price deterioration of small stocks in the aftermath of the burst of the "dot-com bubble". However, whereas these small stocks have not recovered since, big companies could increase their share prices. As a consequence, this could indicate the reversal of the size effect.

The momentum has an annually mean value of 12.587 percent that deviates significantly from its median with 5.368 percent. However, the correlation is high. The momentum is in particular weak in years of crises and one year after. Thus, it is strongly negative in 2008 with 6.90 percent and 2009 with -16.85 percent in the course of the financial crisis. The average mean return per month is 0.57 percent and the median 0.04 percent. The high difference between mean and median again indicates that the returns are negatively skewed.

---

[185] It should be negatively correlated, since $DY = \frac{D}{P}$ which is the reciprocal formation to the other value premium proxies.

[186] See table 13.

Table 11: Summary statistics 1992 - 2011

Years	P/B		P/E		DY [%]		Size [EUR m]		Momentum [%]		Monthly return [%]	
	Mean	Median	Mean	Median	Mean	Median	Mean	Median	Mean	Median	Mean	Median
1992	2,975	2,176	55,445	20,513	2,347	2,275	1179,107	195,823	-2,564	-3,765	-0,723	-0,746
1993	2,511	2,038	47,493	22,779	2,353	2,224	1292,758	195,520	-1,530	1,052	2,417	1,754
1994	2,842	2,212	47,364	25,958	1,881	1,873	1540,276	223,904	20,561	14,645	-0,013	-0,201
1995	2,605	2,006	53,329	21,879	2,074	2,004	1439,826	199,393	-3,777	-4,450	-0,277	-0,427
1996	2,716	1,904	69,816	19,892	2,356	2,186	1580,608	185,303	2,536	0,810	0,456	0,252
1997	5,430	2,218	85,418	23,625	2,071	1,887	2048,979	193,389	20,907	18,383	2,382	1,174
1998	3,703	2,370	101,531	23,688	1,969	1,783	2714,561	203,520	23,394	8,382	1,100	-0,393
1999	3,323	2,133	119,310	20,563	2,531	2,023	2507,124	177,014	12,191	-3,621	0,580	-0,325
2000	4,810	2,231	351,659	21,704	2,698	1,987	2858,642	185,046	18,042	0,667	0,243	-0,309
2001	3,742	1,828	126,803	17,338	2,817	2,013	2209,637	136,060	-7,078	-7,127	-1,735	-1,336
2002	2,667	1,610	85,985	15,679	3,000	2,350	1890,292	125,059	-9,292	-8,004	-2,607	-1,373
2003	2,131	1,450	53,052	14,483	3,031	2,177	1402,074	126,073	-0,143	-1,578	2,810	1,530
2004	2,460	1,670	33,224	18,067	2,237	1,407	1849,376	132,013	47,825	28,111	1,433	0,897
2005	2,498	1,758	39,002	19,029	1,701	1,193	2010,892	123,622	32,707	19,805	2,647	1,444
2006	2,725	1,877	55,692	19,192	1,732	1,142	2253,353	121,338	37,898	21,448	1,855	0,947
2007	2,762	1,993	44,054	17,775	1,773	1,063	2539,336	126,618	22,137	13,618	0,578	-0,099
2008	2,379	1,593	32,426	12,842	2,630	1,895	2027,480	86,260	-6,901	-13,457	-4,113	-3,555
2009	2,562	1,349	28,585	13,083	3,675	2,442	1398,693	72,045	-16,852	-15,021	3,134	1,654
2010	2,564	1,583	39,547	17,713	2,415	1,704	1830,666	96,567	39,053	23,184	1,861	1,006
2011	2,114	1,543	33,284	15,125	2,297	1,810	1972,340	99,214	22,628	14,275	-0,622	-1,018
Mean / Median	2,976	1,877	75,151	19,046	2,379	1,872	1927,301	150,189	12,587	5,368	0,570	0,044
Std. Dev.	8,008		688,152		3,543		6800,889		47,898		10,496	

(Source: Data from Thomson Reuters Datastream)

Figure 5: Development of firm characteristics

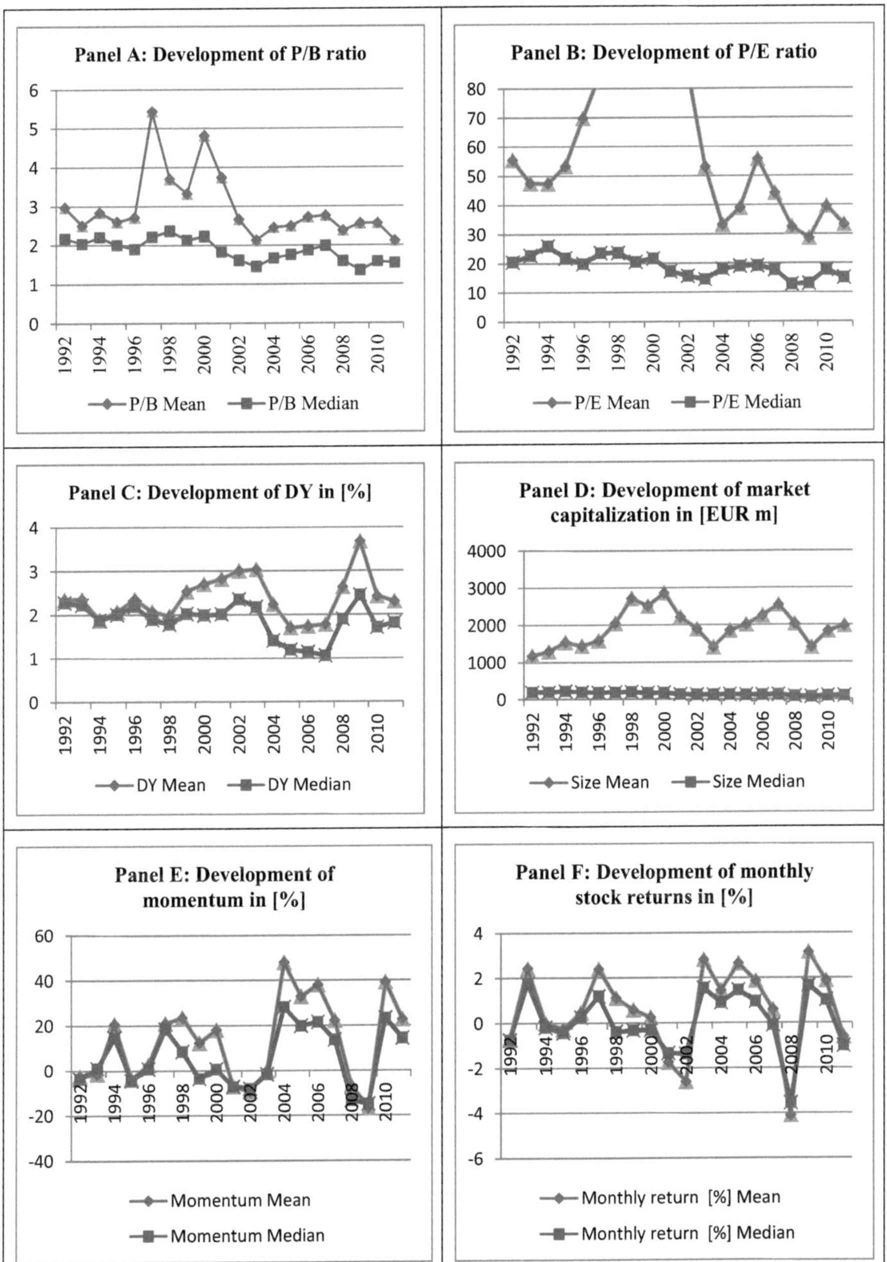

(Source: Data from Thomson Reuters Datastream)

Table 12 shows the average Pearson correlation coefficients. They are computed for each portfolio of stocks every month. Mean correlations are then calculated for each year and finally for the entire time series. Most correlations are rather low. However, there is a stronger positive correlation between P/B and P/E with 0.293. As stated earlier, if the Pearson correlation is applied on yearly medians of P/B and P/E, the correlation is even 0.898.

Table 12: Average Pearson Correlation Coefficients

Pearson Correlation	P/B	P/E	DY	Size	Momentum
P/B	1.000				
P/E	0.294	1.000			
DY	-0.080	-0.074	1.000		
Size	0.010	-0.021	-0.018	1.000	
Momentum	0.125	0.065	-0.086	0.033	1.000

(Source: Data from Thomson Reuters Datastream)

Table 13 shows the average monthly returns with respect to the quintile portfolios and the hedge portfolios. The hedge portfolios consist of three value premium portfolios (low P/B minus high P/B, low P/E minus high P/E, and high DY minus low DY), a size portfolio that is long in big companies and short in small companies (BMS) and a momentum portfolio that is long in high momentum stocks and short in low momentum stocks (UMD). The results are basically consistent with past empirical evidence. The numbers reveal highly significant value premiums. On average, a portfolio that is long in low P/B stocks and short in high P/B stocks, generates a monthly return of 1.59 percent ($t = 7.203$). The P/E hedge return is also highly significant being 3.069 standard errors away from zero. The hedge return of the dividend yield is also significant at the 1%- level. Furthermore, the BMS premium is positive which means that the size effect is negative. However, the mean is close to zero and is therefore not significant. The UMD portfolio yields the highest return with 1.62 percent ($t = 5.583$).

The results seem to be straight forward, since the returns develop with the portfolio, i.e. PF 5 of P/B has a higher return than PF 4, PF 4 has a higher return than PF 3, and so on. My findings are in line with the results of Fama and French and others who propose a value- and a size premium in all markets around the world.[187] I find a highly significant value premium and a negative size premium for the German market between 1992 and 2011.

Table 13: Average monthly returns[188]

	Mean					Hedge-portfolio
	1	2	3	4	5	5 minus 1
P/B	-0.148	0.268	0.495	0.800	1.442	1.590 (7.203) ***
P/E	0.206	0.384	0.711	0.681	0.870	0.664 (3.069) ***
DY	0.122	0.466	0.598	0.705	0.961	0.839 (3.533) ***
Size	0.717	0.336	0.427	0.529	0.837	0.120 (0.578)
Momentum	-0.296	0.268	0.654	0.911	1.321	1.617 (5.583)***
	Median					Hedge-portfolio
	1	2	3	4	5	5 minus 1
P/B	-0.362	-0.027	-0.053	0.181	0.510	0.872
P/E	-0.406	-0.123	0.211	0.235	0.177	0.583
DY	-0.847	-0.257	0.078	0.173	0.541	1.388
Size	-0.183	-0.405	-0.034	0.118	0.502	0.685
Momentum	-0.969	-0.217	0.157	0.368	0.412	1.381
	Std.Dev.					Hedge-portfolio
	1	2	3	4	5	5 minus 1
P/B	10.682	9.421	9.862	9.483	11.377	0.695
P/E	11.325	9.500	8.924	9.172	11.731	0.406
DY	13.312	10.824	8.409	8.481	8.943	-4.369
Size	12.632	11.303	10.006	8.954	7.327	-5.305
Momentum	12.469	9.301	8.532	8.631	10.913	-1.556

(Source: Data from Thomson Reuters Datastream)

Table 14 splits the average monthly hedge portfolio returns on a yearly basis. Both, P/B and P/E hedge portfolios generate average monthly positive returns for most years between 1992 and 2011. Hence, a value strategy yields positive returns in many months. The results further suggest that value strategies based on P/B and P/E work best in years of strong market movements. Hence, a P/B value strategy yielded between 4.83 percent in the aftermath of the "new economy boom" in 2001. With the start of the financial crisis in 2008, such a strategy even yielded 3.963 percent per month in 2009. A value strategy based on dividend yields delivers also positive returns in most years. In particular, the years 2001 and 2002 yielded average returns between 4.33 and 4.38 percent. The BMS strategy also yields positive returns for most years, however, they are very small. Consistent with the DY strategy, an UMD strategy performed best in the years 2001 and 2002 with average monthly returns around 5 percent.

[187] See for example Fama and French (1998), p. 1975.

[188] T-statistics are in Parentheses (* is significant at the 10%-level, ** significant at the 5%-level, and *** significant at the 1%-level).

	Table 14: Hedge-portfolio (5 - 1) average monthly returns				
	P/B	P/E	DY	Size	Mom.
1992	0.949	0.610	0.820	0.332	2.156
1993	2.267	1.427	0.674	1.068	-0.607
1994	0.761	1.023	0.583	-0.763	-0.532
1995	0.641	0.215	0.846	0.736	2.077
1996	-0.026	-0.409	0.321	1.507	2.682
1997	2.309	0.166	-0.923	0.415	0.046
1998	1.516	-0.603	-1.819	-0.619	2.922
1999	1.520	-1.249	-1.807	0.330	2.589
2000	2.057	1.859	2.865	-0.267	-0.557
2001	4.831	3.393	4.327	0.894	4.936
2002	0.373	-0.334	4.378	0.483	5.597
2003	3.176	0.691	1.436	0.414	0.625
2004	0.572	1.549	0.962	-0.542	2.461
2005	1.876	0.983	-1.227	-1.215	1.807
2006	2.135	-0.441	0.041	0.934	0.754
2007	0.419	0.412	1.093	0.590	1.834
2008	-0.249	-0.564	1.047	0.376	3.031
2009	3.963	3.198	1.479	-0.937	-3.132
2010	2.062	1.018	0.802	-0.119	2.299
2011	0.637	0.332	0.879	-1.214	1.363

(Source: Data from Thomson Reuters Datastream)

Figure 6 illustrates the average monthly hedge portfolio returns for Value-, BMS- and UMD-investing. Except of a few years, all strategies generate positive returns.

Figure 6: Monthly average hedge portfolio returns in [%] for value investing, BMS, and UMD

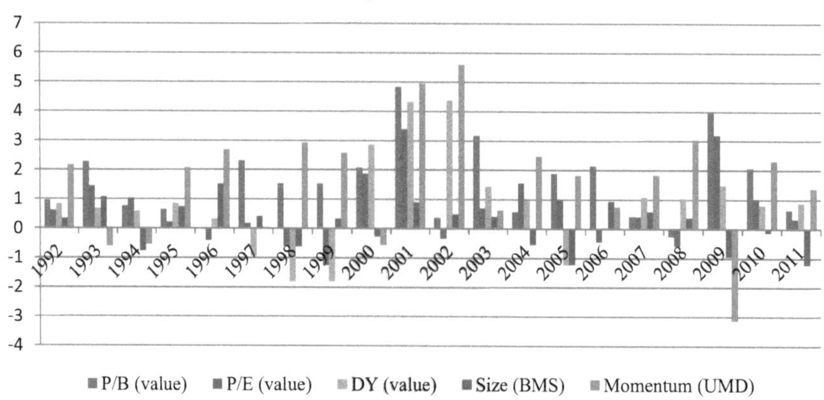

6.3. Seasonality

In this section I will try to figure out, whether there is a month[189] where a hedging strategy performs best. Table 15 shows the average return for each month. It also reveals the excess return to the yearly mean of each hedge characteristic and the t-statistics[190] in parentheses. In January, a P/B hedge strategy outperforms the yearly mean about 1.029 percent, a P/E strategy 0.746 percent, and a DY strategy 0.536 percent. The P/B strategy performs best in April with an excess return of 2.17 percent and is significant at the 1%-level. The worst months are October and December. A P/E strategy yields a significant return in June, whereas July and October seem to be the worst months. In contrast, BMS and UMD strategies are most beneficial in July and October. Therefore, it could be argued that value strategies and UMD as well as BMS strategies are negatively correlated. This is a very interesting finding for professional traders, in particular. Thus, an investor could achieve even higher returns, if he changes his investment strategies during the year based on this pattern. It would be best to follow a value investing strategy in April, and a UMD strategy in July.

There is a bulk of literature that investigates seasonality effects on stock returns. A well documented phenomenon, for example, is the so-called January effect that documents that stocks perform considerable better in January in comparison to the rest of the year.[191] In addition, Heston et al. (1999) find that the size premium (SMB) is significantly higher in January.[192] Agarwal et al. (2011) investigate the returns of hedge funds and find significant higher December returns. They argue that management would have incentives to report better results in December in order to earn a higher performance fee.[193] However, I am not acquainted with any study that analyses seasonality patterns in hedge portfolios formed on firm characteristics, and thus, there is no evidence for these patterns. Thus, no explanations can be given why certain strategies outperform in certain months. However, this should be a interesting issue for future research.

[189] Note that I calculate monthly returns from the 15th of a month to the 15th of the previous month. Thus, for example, the return in August is calculated from the 15th of July to the 15th of August.

[190] The t-statistics have to be considered carefully, since the sample size is very low with 20 observations and 19 degrees of freedom.

[191] See De Bondt and Thaler (1987), p. 559.

[192] See Heston et al. (1999), p. 17 f.

[193] See Agarwal et al. (2011), p. 3281.

Table 15: Returns related to seasonality[194]

	P/B (value)	(+/-) year (t-stat.)	P/E (value)	(+/-) year (t-stat.)	DY (value)	(+/-) year (t-stat.)	Size (BMS)	(+/-) year (t-stat.)	Mom. (UMD)	(+/-) year (t-stat.)
Year	*1.590*		*0.664*		*0.839*		*0.120*		*1.617*	
Jan	2.619	1.029 (1.202)	1.410	0.746 (0.985)	1.375	0.536 (0.582)	-1.133	-1.253 (-1.837)**	0.409	-1.209 (-1.755)**
Feb	0.566	-1.023 (-0.956)	-0.029	-0.693 (-0.567)	-0.070	-0.909 (-0.922)	0.496	0.376 (0.373)	2.039	0.421 (0.395)
Mar	1.751	0.162 (0.200)	-0.014	-0.678 (-0.897)	0.999	0.160 (0.195)	-1.023	-1.143 (-1.145)*	2.773	1.156 (1.226)
Apr	3.760	2.170 (2.44)***	1.799	1.135 (1.231)	2.118	1.279 (1.264)	0.767	0.647 (1.053)	0.839	-0.779 (-0.509)
May	2.034	0.445 (0.602)	1.414	0.751 (1.229)	1.367	0.528 (0.949)	-0.910	-1.030 (-1.404)*	-0.341	-1.958 (-2.125)**
Jun	2.053	0.464 (0.847)	1.377	0.714 (1.535)*	1.195	0.357 (0.435)	-0.500	-0.620 (-1.415)*	2.007	0.389 (0.383)
Jul	0.525	-1.065 (-1.721)*	-0.362	-1.026 (-2.088)**	-0.515	-1.354 (-1.953)**	1.212	1.092 (1.920)**	3.920	2.302 (2.105)**
Aug	2,256	0,666 (1.170)	0.891	0.227 (0.413)	1.178	0.339 (0.544)	-0.452	-0.572 (-0.824)	0.928	-0.689 (-0.902)
Sep	1.907	0.318 (0.614)	1.232	0.568 (1.149)	0.776	-0.063 (-0.099)	-0.149	-0.269 (-0.404)	1.501	-0.116 (-0.139)
Oct	0.163	-1.426 (-2.256)**	-0.781	-1.445 (-2.052)**	0.896	0.057 (0.070)	1.703	1.583 (2.257)**	2.497	0.879 (0.880)
Nov	2.094	0.505 (0.749)	0.551	-0.113 (-0.141)	0.700	-0.139 (-0.187)	0.466	0.346 (0.503)	0.429	-1.189 (-1.297)
Dec	-0.655	-2.244 (-3.19)***	0.478	-0.186 (-0.233)	0.047	-0.792 (-0.721)	0.963	0.843 (1.153)	2.410	0.792 (0.895)

(Source: Data from Thomson Reuters Datastream)

194 T-statistics are in Parentheses (* is significant at the 10%-level, ** significant at the 5%-level, and *** significant at the 1%-level).

Figure 7 and 8 illustrate the seasonal hedge portfolio returns with peaks in April and July. As can be seen, the correlation between the single strategies is the lowest in the month July. Figure 8 shows the seasonal hedge portfolio returns in excess of the equity risk premium r_m[195].

Figure 7: Seasonal hedge portfolio returns

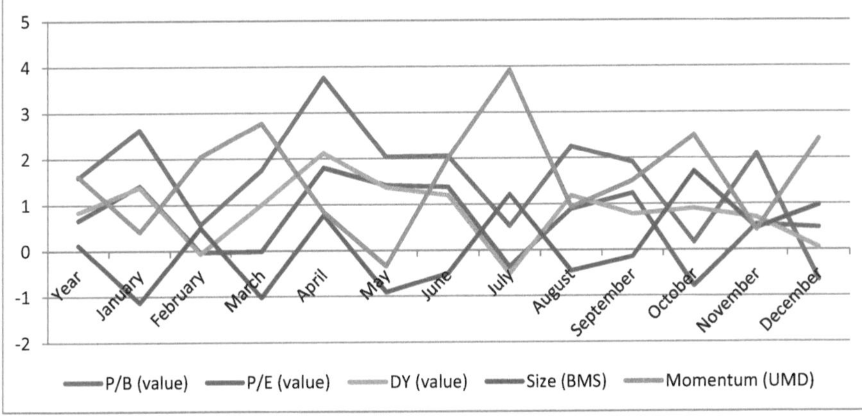

(Source: Data from Thomson Reuters Datastream)

Figure 8: Seasonal hedge portfolio returns in excess of the equity risk premium r(m) (= 0.64 % p.m.)

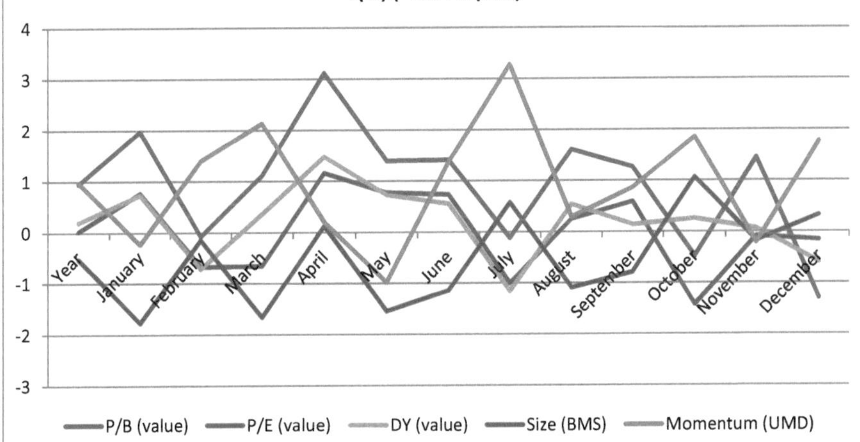

(Source: Data from Thomson Reuters Datastream)

[195] r_m is calculated by the arithmetic mean of the monthly returns of the CDAX Performance Index between January 1992 and December 2011.

6.4. Univariate and multivariate regressions

After calculating and discussing the hedge portfolio returns for the factors P/B, P/E, DY, Size, and Momentum, this section addresses the question whether the single risk factors have a significant influence on expected stock returns and which set of factors faces the highest explanatory power. In a first step, univariate time-series regressions of the following form are run:

$$r_{p,i,t} - r_{f,t} = \propto + \beta' * F_{i,t} + \varepsilon_t \qquad (6.4)$$

$r_{p,i,t}$ denotes the return of the portfolio i in month t with i = 5, $r_{f,t}$ is the risk-free interest rate in month t, $F_{i,t}$ denotes the vector of each factor i (P/B hedge return, P/E hedge return, DY hedge return, BMS, and UMD) at month t, and β' are the factor loadings. Table 16 shows the factor coefficients and the corresponding t-statistics in parentheses for portfolios that are ranked according to the firm characteristics. As can be seen most factors are significant at the one-percent level for many portfolios. However, whereas UMD is significant for all portfolios except of one, the P/E hedge factor and the BMS factor are insignificant for many portfolios. Since it is difficult to identify a general pattern of superior factors considering the univariate regressions, all factors are included in multivariate regressions.

Table 16: Univariate Regressions[196]

Panel A: Univariate regressions on five P/B portfolios

	P/B hedge growth	P/E hedge growth	DY hedge growth	BMS	UMD
PF 1	-0.212 (-2.662) ***	-0.255 (-3.158) ***	-0.621 (-9.815) ***	0.159 (1.870)*	-0.213 (-3.548) ***
PF 2	0.213 (2.792) ***	0.071 (0.900)	-0.338 (-4.936) ***	0.214 (2.636)***	-0.295 (-5.294) ***
PF 3	0.316 (4.002) ***	0.172 (2.088) **	-0.323 (-4.434) ***	0.259 (3.047) ***	-0.295 (-4.989) ***
PF 4	0.433 (5.862) ***	0.313 (4.013) ***	-0.190 (-2.630) ***	0.178 (2.140) **	-0.345 (-6.183) ***
PF 5	0.788 (9.910) ***	0.451 (4.904) ***	-0.218 (-2.512) **	0.086 (0.861)	-0.508 (-7.938) ***

Panel B: Univariate regressions on five P/E portfolios

[196] T-statistics are in Parentheses (* is significant at the 10%-level, ** significant at the 5%-level, and *** significant at the 1%-level).

	P/B hedge	P/E hedge	DY hedge	BMS	UMD
PF 1	-0.092 (-1.052)	-0.417 (-4.900) ***	-0.700 (-10.336) ***	0.117 (1.259)	-0.252 (-3.892) ***
PF 2	0.209 (2.830) ***	0.071 (0.932)	-0.347 (-5.253) ***	0.186 (2.359) **	-0.267 (-4.891) ***
PF 3	0.318 (4.337) ***	0.180 (2.351) **	-0.243 (-3.527) ***	0.263 (3.322) ***	-0.297 (-5.436) ***
PF 4	0.520 (6.713) ***	0.337 (4.049) ***	-0.163 (-2.101) **	0.238 (2.699) ***	-0.371 (-6.228) ***
PF 5	0.586 (7.053) ***	0.583 (6.838) ***	-0.235 (-2.814) ***	0.094 (0.967)	-0.470 (-7.505)***

Panel C: Univariate regressions on five DY portfolios

	P/B hedge	P/E hedge	DY hedge	BMS	UMD
PF 1	0.087 (0.832)	-0.129 (-1.208)	-0.954 (-12.721) ***	-0.011 (-0.101)	-0.415 (-5.532) ***
PF 2	0.215 (2.567) **	0.023 (0.268)	-0.418 (-5.643) ***	0.234 (2.629) ***	-0.352 (-5.831) ***
PF 3	0.294 (4.160) ***	0.182 (2.462) **	-0.210 (-3.150) ***	0.301 (4.002) ***	-0.237 (-4.425) ***
PF 4	0.391 (5.488) ***	0.246 (3.262) ***	-0.151 (-2.169) **	0.244 (3.090) ***	-0.247 (-4.465) ***
PF 5	0.554 (7.658) ***	0.431 (5.559) ***	0.046 (0.614)	0.131 (1.539)	-0.405 (-7.291) ***

Panel D: Univariate regressions on five Size portfolios

	P/B hedge	P/E hedge	DY hedge	BMS	UMD
PF 1	0.357 (4.950) ***	0.174 (2.267) **	-0.371 (-5.604) ***	-0.293 (-3.741) ***	-0.349 (-6.563) ***
PF 2	0.357 (4.284) ***	0.167 (1.902) *	-0.405 (-5.331) ***	0.019 (0.211)	-0.388 (-6.368) ***
PF 3	0.302 (3.736) ***	0.136 (1.615)	-0.330 (-4.439) ***	0.120 (1.359)	-0.356 (-6.036) ***
PF 4	0.229 (2.714) ***	0.123 (1.415)	-0.321 (-4.170) ***	0.346 (3.916) ***	-0.337 (-5.471) ***
PF 5	0.293 (3.519) ***	0.152 (1.758) *	-0.262 (-3.383) ***	0.707 (9.024) ***	-0.225 (-3.556) ***

Panel E: Univariate regressions on five Momentum portfolios

	P/B hedge	P/E hedge	DY hedge	BMS	UMD
PF 1	0.523 (4.699) ***	0.287 (2.452) **	-0.530 (-5.176) ***	0.031 (0.254)	-0.919 (-14.022) ***
PF 2	0.441 (5.835) ***	0.269 (3.337) ***	-0.229 (-3.102) ***	0.147 (1.720) *	-0.435 (-7.495) ***
PF 3	0.315 (4.261) ***	0.184 (2.579) **	-0.184 (-2.825) ***	0.216 (2.908) ***	-0.269 (-5.261) ***
PF 4	0.249 (3.718) ***	0.115 (1.652)	-0.231 (-3.723) ***	0.231 (3.226) ***	-0.112 (-2.160) **
PF 5	0.013 (0.150)	-0.103 (-1.178)	-0.516 (-7.08) ***	0.272 (3.020) ***	0.081 (1.240)

(Source: Data from Thomson Reuters Datastream)

Applying multivariate regressions, eight different models (M) are tested in order to identify the one that has the best explanatory power. The eight models are built as follows:

$$\boldsymbol{M1}: r_{p,i,t} - r_{f,t} = \alpha_i + \beta_{mkt,i} RMRF_t + \varepsilon_{p,t} \quad (6.5)$$

$$\boldsymbol{M2}: r_{p,i,t} - r_{f,t} = \alpha_i + \beta_{mkt,i} RMRF_t + \beta_{P/B,i} P/B_t + \beta_{BMS,i} BMS_t + \varepsilon_{p,t} \quad (6.6)$$

$$\boldsymbol{M3}: r_{p,i,t} - r_{f,t} = \alpha_i + \beta_{mkt,i} RMRF_t + \beta_{P/B,i} P/B_t + \beta_{BMS,i} BMS_t + \beta_{UMD,i} UMD_t + \varepsilon_{p,t} \quad (6.7)$$

$$\boldsymbol{M4}: r_{p,i,t} - r_{f,t} = \alpha_i + \beta_{mkt,i} RMRF_t + \beta_{P/B,i} P/B_t + \beta_{P/E,i} P/E_t + \varepsilon_{p,t} \quad (6.8)$$

$$\boldsymbol{M5}: r_{p,i,t} - r_{f,t} = \alpha_i + \beta_{mkt,i} RMRF_t + \beta_{P/B,i} P/B_t + \beta_{P/E,i} P/E_t + \beta_{UMD,i} UMD_t + \varepsilon_{p,t} \quad (6.9)$$

$$\boldsymbol{M6}: r_{p,i,t} - r_{f,t} = \alpha_i + \beta_{mkt,i} RMRF_t + \beta_{P/B,i} P/B_t + \beta_{DY,i} DY_t + \varepsilon_{p,t} \quad (6.10)$$

$$\boldsymbol{M7}: r_{p,i,t} - r_{f,t} = \alpha_i + \beta_{mkt,i} RMRF_t + \beta_{P/B,i} P/B_t + \beta_{DY,i} DY_t + \beta_{BMS,i} BMS_t + \beta_{UMD,i} UMD_t + \varepsilon_{p,t} \quad (6.11)$$

$$\boldsymbol{M8}: r_{p,i,t} - r_{f,t} = \alpha_i + \beta_{mkt,i} RMRF_t + \beta_{P/B,i} P/B_t + \beta_{P/E,i} P/E_t + \beta_{DY,i} DY_t + \beta_{BMS,i} BMS_t + \beta_{UMD,i} UMD_t + \varepsilon_{p,t} \quad (6.12)$$

Table 17 shows the different coefficients of determinations (adjusted R-squared = R^2) for all portfolios. The model M1 with the market factor RMRF represents the standard CAPM. It has an explanatory power between 0.37 and 0.875 at a mean of 0.636. Extending M1 to a three-factor model M2[197], increases the mean R^2 to 0.764. Adding the momentum factor UMD gives M3 which has a mean explanatory power of 0.778. These results are consistent with the findings of Hanauer et al. (2012) who state that the three-factor model considerable increases the explanatory power in comparison to the CAPM, whereas an additional momentum factor had only a marginal effect.[198] Artmann et al. (2011) propose that a four-factor model that contains the market factor, a P/B-, P/E-, and a Momentum factor (corresponds to M5) does the best job in explaining expected returns. A five-factor model (M7) performs better with a mean R^2 of 0.791, however, the additional explanatory power is small. Evaluating these results, it can be concluded that the Fama and French three factor model does a good job in explaining expected stock returns, since improvements due to additional factors are marginal.

Table 17: Explanatory power of different sets of models[199]

	Panel A: Adjusted R²s of models ranked to P/B				
Model	**PF 1**	**PF 2**	**PF 3**	**PF 4**	**PF5**
M1	0.611	0.702	0.732	0.669	0.589
M2	0.796	0.761	0.791	0.781	0.851
M3	0.799	0.761	0.790	0.781	0.853
M4	0.692	0.703	0.748	0.734	0.775
M5	0.715	0.715	0.751	0.742	0.792
M6	0.740	0.718	0.761	0.728	0.811
M7	0.806	0.761	0.790	0.781	0.858
M8	0.806	0.761	0.796	0.795	0.859

[197] M2 is similar to the Fama and French three-factor model.
[198] See Hanauer et al. (2012), p. 2 f.
[199] T-statistics are in Parentheses (* is significant at the 10%-level, ** significant at the 5%-level, and *** significant at the 1%-level).

Model	PF 1	PF 2	PF 3	PF 4	PF5
	Panel B: Adjusted R^2s of models ranked to P/E				
M1	0.638	0.693	0.744	0.685	0.568
M2	0.753	0.761	0.801	0.802	0.739
M3	0.7753	0.761	0.801	0.802	0.745
M4	0.700	0.694	0.766	0.767	0.724
M5	0.723	0.701	0.771	0.772	0.745
M6	0.726	0.715	0.768	0.765	0.681
M7	0.782	0.761	0.800	0.803	0.8745
M8	0.817	0.762	0.809	0.807	0.831

Model	PF 1	PF 2	PF 3	PF 4	PF5
	Panel C: Adjusted R^2s of models ranked to DY				
M1	0.572	0.696	0.737	0.676	0.549
M2	0.747	0.755	0.775	0.752	0.714
M3	0.752	0.761	0.774	0.754	0.719
M4	0.576	0.696	0.758	0.724	0.683
M5	0.615	0.720	0.758	0.723	0.696
M6	0.805	0.721	0.755	0.721	0.672
M7	0.861	0.763	0.774	0.757	0.768
M8	0.865	0.762	0.781	0.761	0.774

Model	PF 1	PF 2	PF 3	PF 4	PF5
	Panel D: Adjusted R^2s of models ranked to Size				
M1	0.462	0.569	0.629	0.706	0.875
M2	0.862	0.721	0.732	0.730	0.891
M3	0.861	0.723	0.734	0.736	0.891
M4	0.502	0.591	0.641	0.710	0.885
M5	0.53	0.615	0.661	0.724	0.886
M6	0.595	0.616	0.660	0.710	0.882
M7	0.863	0.729	0.733	0.735	0.892
M8	0.867	0.751	0.734	0.739	0.895

	Panel E: Adjusted R²s of models ranked to Momentum				
Model	PF 1	PF 2	PF 3	PF 4	PF5
M1	0.573	0.653	0.669	0.655	0.614
M2	0.729	0.777	0.733	0.697	0.667
M3	0.878	0.793	0.732	0.724	0.778
M4	0.603	0.709	0.697	0.666	0.622
M5	0.827	0.747	0.701	0.667	0.687
M6	0.659	0.718	0.697	0.672	0.655
M7	0.884	0.792	0.733	0.723	0.789
M8	0.886	0.795	0.736	0.725	0.793

(Source: Data from Thomson Reuters Datastream)

7. Conclusion

Based on a "free of survivorship-bias" sample of German stocks listed at the Frankfurt stock exchange, the study investigated the ability of hedge portfolio formation structures, built of three value premium proxies (P/B, P/E, and DY), the size factor, and the technical momentum factor, to generate excess returns in the period 1992 to 2011. I found significant evidence for a value premium as proposed by Fama and French and others. The P/B hedge portfolio yields an average return of 1.59 percent per month, the P/E hedge portfolio 0.664 percent, and a portfolio formation approach ranked on DY delivers a return of 0.839. These returns considerable exceed the returns of comparable studies.[200] This may be due to a different applied methodology, in particular regarding the frequency of portfolio rebalancing. Evaluating these numbers, the P/B proxy seems to be the superior one in exploiting asset pricing anomalies.

Furthermore, the study confirmed the evidence from recent empirical papers regarding the reversal of the size effect. In this study, the size effect is negative, however not significant. Hedge portfolios that are grouped relating to Momentum, yield the highest average returns of 1.617 percent per month. Therefore, the implementation of a technical firm characteristic seems to be beneficial in an asset pricing context.

Investigating the seasonality of hedge portfolio returns revealed surprising results. Whereas value strategies performed worst in July, a momentum strategy or a size strategy achieved

[200] Artmann et al. (2011) find corresponding monthly hedge portfolio returns of 0.900 percent for P/B and 0.991 percent for P/E.

significant excess returns in the month July. Although these findings should not be assessed too high,[201] they certainly could be interesting for professional investors who are flexible in changing their investment strategy during the year. The search for explanations why certain strategies perform better in some months remains an issue for future research.

Finally, I applied multivariate regressions on different sets of risk factors. The main finding is that the Fama and French three factor model does a good job in explaining expected stock returns. An additional momentum factor or dividend yield factor, increases the explanatory power only slightly.

[201] The observation period is very short with only 20 observations and 19 degrees of freedom.

Reference list

Agarwal, V., Daniel, N.D., and Naik N.Y. (2011), Do Hedge Funds Manage Their Reported Returns?, Review of Financial Studies, Vol. 24, No. 10, pp. 3281-3320.

Amihud, Y. (2002), Illiquidity and stock returns: cross-section and time-series effects, Journal of Financial Markets, Vol. 5, No. 1, pp. 31-56.

Ammann, M. and Steiner, M. (2008), Risk Factors for the Swiss Stock Market, Swiss Journal of Economics and Statistics, Vol. 144, No. 1, pp. 1-35.

Artmann, S., Finter, P., and Kempf, A. (2011), Determinants of expected stock Returns: Large sample evidence from the German Market, CFR Working Paper, No. 10-01, University Cologne, pp. 1-37.

Athanassakos, G. (2011), The Performance, Pervasiveness and Determinants of Value Premium in Different US Exchanges: 1986-2006, Journal of Investment Management, Vol. 9, pp. 33-73.

Ball, R. (1978), Anomalies in Relationships between Securities' Yield and Yield-Surrogates, Journal of Financial Economics, Vol. 6, pp. 103-126.

Ballwieser, W. (2007), Unternehmensbewertung: Prozeß, Methoden und Probleme, 2nd edition, Stuttgart.

Banz, R. W. (1981), The Relationship Between Return And Market Value Of Common Stocks, Journal of Financial Economics, Vol. 9, No. 1, pp. 3-18.

Barbee, W. C., Mukherji, S., and Raines, G. A. (1996), Do Sales-Price and Debt-Equity explain Stock Returns better than Book-Market and Firm Size?, Financial Analysts Journal, Vol. 52, No. 2, pp. 56-60.

Barber, B. M. and Lyon, J. D. (1997), Firm Size, Book-to-Market Ratio, and Security Returns: A Holdout Sample of Financial Firms, Journal of Finance, Vol. 52, No. 2, pp. 875-883.

Basu, S. (1983), The relationship between earnings yield, market value, and return for NYSE common stocks: Further evidence, Journal of Financial Economics Vol. 12, pp. 129-156.

Benkert, C. (2004), Default Risk in Bond and Credit Derivatives Markets, Frankfurt (Main).

Berk, J. B. (2000), Sorting out Sorts, Journal of Finance, Vol. 55, No. 1, pp. 407-428.

Bhandari, L. C. (1988), Debt/Equity ratio and expected common stock returns: Empirical evidence, Journal of Finance Vol. 43, pp. 507-528.

Black, F. and Scholes, M. (1974), The effects of dividend yield and dividend policy on common stock prices and returns, Journal of Financial Economics, Vol. 1, No. 1, pp. 1-22.

Breen, W. J. and Korajczyk, R. A. (1993), On Selection Biases in Book-to-Market Based Tests of Asset Pricing Models, Working Paper, Northwestern University.

Brennan, M. J. (1970), Taxes, Market Valuation and Corporate Financial Policy, National Tax Journal, Vol. 23, pp. 417-427.

Carhart, M. M., (1997), On Persistence of Mutual Fund Performance, Journal of Finance, Vol. 52, No. 1, pp. 57-82.

Chan, L. K. C., Hamao, J., and Lakonishok, Josef (1991), Fundamentals and Stock Returns in Japan, Jounal of Finance, Vol. 46, No. 5, pp. 1739-1764.

Chan, L. K. C., Jegadeesh, N., and Lakonishok, J. (1995), Evaluating the Performance of value versus growth stocks – The impact of selection bias, Journal of Financial Economics, Vol. 38, pp. 269 – 296.

Cummins, J. D. and Trainar, P. (2009), Securitization, Insurance and Reinsurance, Journal of Risk and Insurance, Vol. 76, S. 463-492.

Cunningham, L. A. (2004), What is Value Investing?, New York.

Damodaran, A. (2008), Equity Risk Premiums (ERP): Determinants, Estimation and Implications, Working Paper, Stern School of Business.

Daniel, K., Grinblatt, M., Titman, S., and Wermers, R. (1997), Measuring Mutual Fund Performance with Characteristic-based Benchmarks, Journal of Finance, Vol. 52, No. 3, pp. 1035-1058.

Davis, J. L. (1994), The Cross-Section of realized Stock Returns: The Pre-Compustat Evidence, Journal of Finance, Vol. 49, No. 5, pp. 1579-1593.

De Bondt, W. F. M. and Thaler, R. (1985), Does the Stock Market overreact?, Journal of Finance, Vol. 40, No. 3, pp. 793-805.

Dimson, E. and Marsh, P. (1999), Murphy's Law and Market Anomalies, Journal of Portfolio Management, Vol. 23, pp. 53-69.

Dörschell, A., Franken, L., Schulte, J., and Brütting, C. (2008), Ableitung CAPM-basierter Risikozuschläge bei der Unternehmensbewertung – eine kritische Analyse ausgewählter Problemkreise im Rahmen von IDW S1 i.d.F. 2008, Wirtschaftsprüfung, No. 24, pp. 1152-1162.

Drukarczyk, J. (2003): Unternehmensbewertung, 4th edition, München.

Easton, P. D. (2004), PE ratios, PEG ratios, and estimating the implied expected Rate of Return on Equity capital, Accounting Review, Vol. 79, No. 1, pp. 73-95.

Eberhart, A. C., Maxwell, W. F., and Siddique, A. (2004), An examination of long-term abnormal Stock Returns and Operating Performance following R&D Increases, Journal of Finance, Vol. 59, No. 2, pp. 623-650.

Fama, E. F. (1998), Market efficiency, long-term Returns, and behavioral finance, Journal of Financial Economics, Vol. 49, pp. 283-306.

Fama, E. F. and French, K. R. (1988), Dividend yields and expected Stock Returns, Journal of Financial Economics, Vol. 22, pp. 3-25.

Fama, E. F. and French, K. R. (1992), The cross-section of expected Stock returns, Journal of Finance, Vol. 67, No. 2, pp. 427-465.

Fama, E. F. and French, K. R. (1993), Common risk factors in the Returns on stocks and bonds, Journal of Financial Economics, Vol. 33, pp. 3-56.

Fama, E. F. and French, K. R. (1996), The CAPM is Wanted, Dead or Alive, Journal of Finance, Vol. 51, No. 5, pp. 1947-1958.

Fama, E. F. and French, K. R. (1998), Value versus Growth: The International Evidence, Journal of Finance, Vol. 53, No. 6, pp. 1975-1999.

Fama, E. F. and French, K. R. (2010), Size, Value, and Momentum in international Stock Returns, Working paper, Draft Nov. 2010.

Fernandez, P., Aguirreamalloa, J., and Avendano, L. C. (2011), Market Risk Premium used in 56 Countries in 2011: A Survey with 6,014 Answers (April 25, 2011), pp. 1-14.

Flannery, M. J. and Protopapadakis, A. A. (2002), Macroeconomic Factors do influence aggregate Stock Returns, Review of Financial Studies, Vol. 15, No. 3, pp. 751-782,

Geginat, J., Morath, B., Wittmann, R., and Knüsel, P. (2006), Kapitalkosten als strategisches Entscheidungskriterium, Roland Berger Research, pp. 1-34.

Geske, R. and Roll, R. (1983), The Fiscal and Monetary Linkage between Stock Returns and Inflation, Journal of Finance, Vol. 38, No. 1, pp. 1-33.

Gharghori, P., Stryjkowski, S., and Veeraraghavan, M. (2007), Value versus growth: Australian evidence, Working Paper, Monash University, pp. 1-27.

Graham, B. and Zweig, J. (2003), The Intelligent Investor: The Definitive Book on Value Investing, New York.

Greenwald, B. C. N., Kahn, J., Sonkin, P. D., and Biema, M. (2001), Value Investing from Graham to Buffet and beyond, New Jersey.

Griffin, J. M. (2002), Are the Fama and French Factors Global or Country Specific?, Review of Financial Studies, Vol. 15, No. 3, pp. 783-803.

Gulen, H., Xing, Y., and Zhang, L. (2008), Value versus Growth: Time- varying expected Stock Returns, Working Paper, University of Michigan.

Hanauer, M., Kaserer, C., and Rapp, M.S. (2012), Risikofaktoren und Multifaktormodelle für den Deutschen Aktienmarkt, CEFS Working Paper, 01-2011.

Heston, S. L., Rouwenhorst, K. G., and Wessels, R. E. (1999), The Role of Beta and Size in the Cross-section of European Stock Returns, European Financial Management, Vol. 5, No. 1, pp. 9-27.

Horowitz, J. L., Loughran, T., and Savin, N. E. (2000), Three analyses of the firm size premium, Journal of Empirical Finance, Vol. 7, pp. 143-153.

Jegadeesh, N. and Titman, S. (1993), Returns to buying Winners and selling Losers: Implications for Stock Market Efficiency, Journal of Finance, Vol. 48, No. 1, pp. 65-91.

Koch, S. (2010), Illiquidity and Stock Returns: Evidence from the German Stock Market, Working Paper, University of Bonn.

Kothari, S. P., Shanken, J., and Sloan, R. G. (1995), Another look at the Cross-section of expected Stock Returns, Journal of Finance, Vol. 50. No. 1, pp. 185-224.

Kothari, S. P. and Shanken, J. (1997), Book-to-Market, Dividend yield, and expected market returns: A time-series Analysis, Journal of Financial Economics, Vol. 44, No. 2, pp. 169-203.

Lakonishok, J., Shleifer, A., and Vishny, R. W. (1994), Contrarian Investment, Extrapolation, and Risk, Journal of Finance, Vol. 49, No. 5, pp. 1541-1578.

Lintner, J. (1965), The Valuation of Risk Assets and the Selection of Risky Investments in Stock Portfolios and Capital Budgets, Review of Economics and Statistics, Vol. 47, No. 1, pp. 13-37.

Lowe, J. (1996), Value Investing Made Easy, New York.

Lyon, J. D., Barber, B. M., and Tsai, C.-L. (1999), Improved Methods for Tests of Long-Run abnormal Stock Returns, Journal of Finance, Vol. 54, No. 1, pp. 165-201.

Markowitz, H. M. (1952), Portfolio Selection, Journal of Finance, Vol. 7, No. 1, pp. 77-91.

Markowitz, H. M. (2005), Market Efficiency: A theoretical Distinction and So What?, Financial Analysts Journal, Vol. 61, No. 5, pp. 17-30.

Martin, F. K., Hansen, N., Link, S., and Nicoski, R. (2008), Benjamin Graham and the power of growth stocks: lost growth stock strategies from the father of value investing, New York.

Modigliani, F. and Miller, M. H. (1958), The Cost of Capital, Corporate Finance and the Theory of Investment, American Economic Review, Vol. 48, No. 3, pp. 261-297.

Montier, J. (2009), Value Investing – Tools and Techniques for intelligent Investment, New York.

Naranjo, A., Nimalendram, M., and Ryngaert, M. (1998), Stock Returns, Dividend Yields, and Taxes, Journal of Finance, Vol. 53, No. 6, pp. 2029-2057.

Naumer, H.-J., Nacken, D., Scheurer, S., and Goebel, S. (2009), Value oder Growth – mehr als eine Stilfrage, Allianz Global Investors, PortfolioPraxis: Akademie.

Nguyen, T, (2008), Handbuch der wert- und risikoorientierten Steuerung von Versicherungsunternehmen, Karlsruhe.

Pastor, L. (2003), Liquidity Risk and Expected Stock Returns, Journal of Political Economy, Vol. 11, No. 3, pp. 642-684.

Perridon, L. and Steiner, M. (1993), Finanzwirtschaft der Unternehmen, 7th edition, München.

Peters, D. (1991), Valuing a growth stock, Journal of Portfolio Management, Vol. 17, No. 3, pp. 49-51.

Reese, R. and Wiese, J. (2005), Die kapitalmarktorientierte Ermittlung des Basiszinses für die Unternehmensbewertung – Operationalisierung, Schätzverfahren und Anwendungsprobleme, Working Paper, München.

Rosenberg, B., Kenneth R., and Lanstein, R. (1985), Persuasive evidence of market inefficiency, Journal of Portfolio Management, Vol. 11, pp. 9-17.

Rouwenhorst, K. G. (1999), Local Return Factors and Turnover in Emerging Stock Markets, Journal of Finance, Vol. 54, pp. 1439-1464.

Schiereck, D., De Bondt, W., and Weber, M. (1999), Contrarian and Momentum Strategies in Germany, Financial Analysts Journal, Vol. 55, No. 6, pp. 104-116.

Schulz, A. and Stehle, R. (2002), Buchwert-Marktwert-Verhältnis, Size und Beta als Erklärungsvariable für die Renditen deutscher Aktien, Working Paper, Humboldt Universität Berlin.

Sharpe,W. F. (1964), Capital Asset Prices: A Theory of Market Equilibrium under Conditions of Risk, Journal of Finance, Vol. 19, No. 3, pp. 425-442.

Shen, G. and Huang, X. (2011), Advanced Research on Computer Science and Information Engineering, Part 2, International Conference, CSIE 2011, Zhengzhou (China).

Sheu, H.-J., Wu, S., and Ku, K.-P. (1998), Cross-Sectional Relationships between Stock Returns and Market beta, Trading Volume, and Sales-to-Price in Taiwan, International Review of Fianancial Analysis, Vol. 7, No. 1, pp. 1-18.

Shleifer, A. and Vishny, R. W. (1997), The Limits of Arbitrage, Journal of Finance, Vol. 52, No. 1, pp, 35-55.

Stattman, D. (1980), Book values and stock returns, The Chicago MBA, Journal of Selected Papers, Vol. 4, pp. 25-45.

Stehle, R. E. (1997), Der Size-Effekt am deutschen Aktienmarkt, Zeitschrift für Bankrecht und Bankwirtschaft, Vol. 9, pp. 237 - 260.

Stehle, R. E. (1999), Renditevergleich von Aktien und festverzinslichen Wertpapieren auf Basis des Dax und des REXP, Working Paper, Humboldt Universität, Berlin.

Stehle, R. E. (2004), Die Festlegung der Risikoprämie von Aktien im Rahmen der Schätzung des Wertes von börsennotierten Kapitalgesellschaften, Wirtschaftsprüfung, No. 17., pp. 906-927.

Svensson, L. E. O. (1994), Estimating and Interpreting forward interest rates: Sweden 1992-1994, NBER Working Paper, No. 4871, pp. 1-49.

van Dijk, M. A. (2011), Is Size Dead? A Review of the Size Effect in Equity Returns, Journal of Banking & Finance, Vol. 35, No. 12, pp. 3263-3274.

Watrin, C., Stahlberg, G., and Kappenberg, C. (2011), Der Einfluss des Wochentags auf den Betafaktor – Eine empirische Analyse anhand ausgewählter Kapitalmärkte, Corporate Finance Fachportal vom 11.04.2011, No. 3, pp. 176-194.

Whitman, M. J. (1999), Value Investing: A balanced Approach, New York.

Wiese, J. (2006), Unternehmensbewertung mit dem Nachsteuer-CAPM?, Working Paper, München.

Zhang, L. (2005), The Value premium, Journal of Finance, Vol. 60, No. 1, pp. 67-103.

Ziegler, A., Eberts, E., Schröder, M., Schulz, A., and Stehle, R. (2007), Multifaktormodelle zur Erklärung deutscher Aktienrenditen: Eine empirische Analyse, Working Paper, No. 03-45, Centre for European Economic Research.